BIBLE PROMISES

FOR THE

HEALING

JOURNEY

by

Lana L. Bateman

Barbour Books
Westwood, New Jersey

Scripture quotations from the New Revised Standard Version Bible, copyright 1989 by the Division of Christian Education of the National Council of the Churches of Christ in the USA. Used by permission.

Scripture taken from the New American Standard Bible, © 1960, 1962, 1963, 1968, 1971, 1972, 1973, 1975, 1977 by The Lockman Foundation. Used by permission.

ISBN   1-55748-236-5 — Softbound
ISBN   1-55748-255-1 — Hardbound

Published by **Barbour and Company, Inc.**
      P.O. Box 1219
      Westwood, New Jersey 07675

Cover illustration / design by Drew Winebrenner

Typesetting by Typetronix, Inc., Cape Coral, Florida

Printed in the United States of America

With love and admiration, I dedicate this book of Bible promises to my mother-in-law, Aline. She has been an inspiration to me these past few years, perhaps in ways she will never know. I have watched her courageous fight for life and have marveled at her ability to survive against all odds.

As I write this book, she is very near Heaven. May our Lord grant her tender mercy as she steps from this life into the beauty and peace of His loving presence. Knowing that she will be there makes the Kingdom of Heaven even more precious to me.

CONTENTS

PREFACE

Bible Promises for the Healing Journey has been written to comfort and encourage those who are yearning for wholeness. At Philippian Ministries we are finding that growing numbers are working through pain to release the past wounds of abuse, victimization, and dysfunctional families. Many have been sexually molested or have suffered through the pain of growing up with an alcoholic family member. This text, incidentally, is the perfect companion to any type of recovery or Twelve Step program.

The following verses have been compiled by victims who, through the grace of our Lord, are walking the healing journey. We desire for you to know the comfort with which He has comforted us as He spoke to the wounded child of our hearts through His word.

Christ Jesus has called each of us to come unto Him even as a little child, yet so many of us faced terrible distortions as children. In light of these scars we have been unable to trust our Lord with the heart of a child, or to see Him through the eyes of a child. Often in the healing process our hearts cry out, "Why?" or "What would God have me do with this anger?" or "Can I ever rest from the pain long enough to find the trusting heart of the child I was never allowed to be?"

I'd like to share a poem I wrote after identifying my own victimization and the weeping little one inside.

A FRAGILE HOPE

Safe place . . .

       safe place . . .

              safe place . . .

A curly headed cherub

       is crying out for rest . . .

          grown tired of the weight of woman's soul.

Now stretching on the tips of toes

       full-panicked from the strain,

          too small to bear a burden this intense.

How can she stay up on her toes that long . . .

          with body now so large

             and hair so gray?

No wonder she's grown weary balanced there,

       for how much can a little one endure . . .

          of weight so overwhelmingly unfair?

And where have toys of passing childhood gone . . .

       when tiny legs could dance with sheer delight

          and feet were weary only from one's play?

Can pain erase such joys

       with one broad stroke . . .

         to leave behind the shock of middle-age . . .

          of wrinkled hands

              and

                 eyes that cannot see?

Or does it turn in time to fragile hope

         for ravaged childlike heart

           to see through blooming eyes

     that elderly facades need not be graves

          and tiny feet can grow . . .

              to dance again.

These words express the beginning of a new and fragile ability to recognize the reality of the past and present pain with a dawning desire to hope again. Oh, how that little one in me needed to see Jesus and feel His touch!

I found that touch in the words of my God as I traveled the healing journey. May His words on these following pages both comfort, encourage, and grant you journeys' mercies as they have for me and the many others who courageously traveled before you.

> Thou hast turned for me my
> mourning into dancing;
> Thou has loosed my sackcloth
> and girded me with gladness
> That my soul may sing praise
> to Thee, and not be silent.
> O Lord my God, I will give
> thanks to Thee forever.
>
> *Psalm 30:11-12 (ASV)*

With grateful heart I acknowledge the assistance of the following.

I thank friend and coworker, Kay Kocour, who dedicated countless hours typing the manuscript and sharing special insights from her own personal healing journey. The closing poem in this book (p. 119) is one of her special contributions.

Susan Borgstrom generously volunteered her editing skills; her friendship and encouragement helped give me the impetus to complete this work.

I thank Kathy Blume and all who prayed without ceasing that a book such as this might be made available to God's wounded children.

A special word of thanks goes to Dr. Jim Rockwood who, through the grace of God, has labored with tender compassion through the most difficult hours of my ongoing process to seek the Beloved.

Most importantly, I thank my Savior who never ceases to call me forth from the dark places of pain into His marvelous light.

LANA L. BATEMAN

1
PREPARATION

No one is foolish enough to begin a journey without having in mind a destination. Likewise, to travel without certain necessities such as money and clothing might seem equally ridiculous. The avenue to healing is no different. One must be prepared before embarking on the voyage to wholeness.

First you must consider the price of the trip. Can you even afford to go? Are you willing to pay for the privilege of taking such an important step? There will be pain along the way, and for some there might be a need for professional help. Are you willing to pay the cost for whatever might be required?

What resources should you take to make the journey as pleasant and safe as possible? An empty suitcase won't take you far, but you can't hope to move well from place to place with large numbers of baggage. Given the importance of this trip, you must take only the most valuable and suitable assets to help you along the way.

Many of you are just beginning the healing journey; others have been traveling for some time. Even if you are just thinking of making such an expedition, the following words from our Lord will help you count the cost, and they will fill your luggage with the resources that will be critical in the days to come. Whether your past abuse was emotional, physical, sexual, alcoholic, or ritualistic, the way to wholeness involves certain choices. Once you have counted the cost, it is time to pack your bag.

You will first need to resolve in your heart that you will finish the trip you begin. When the going gets tough, you must be able to look back to the firm determination that led you to choose this difficult but rewarding path.

You will require a passport of courage. Courage is born out of the heart of our Lord. It is in Him that you find the courage to go on even when the going seems impossible. When you face the truth that you have no true courage of your own, you begin to reach for His strength and courage to be steadfast in the face of danger. You find that you can overcome the impossible as you draw from Him.

Your itinerary will include a firm commitment. Are you committed to the process of healing? Have you made a pledge in your heart that by God's grace you will become whole? Are you willing to go wherever He might lead you to obtain that freedom? Is this the call He has placed on your life at this time? If all answers to these questions are "Yes," then you are indeed ready to travel this road.

You will need support from many ports of call. Support is an important part of any healing process. Friends and church are fine, but the supportive promises and assurances that can only come from God are without equal. No healing process can truly bring freedom without the support of our Lord.

Whether you are counseling with a friend, pastor, lay person, or professional, you will need His special support as you grow in wholeness. He alone can truly prepare you for the journey ahead. He longs to give you water when you thirst, bread when you hunger, and loving compassion when you hurt.

You will need many changes of perseverance. That involves a longing to keep going no matter what might occur. You will need tenacity to hold to the course without giving way. Through shame and fear, pain and tears, longing and resolution you will possess such determination that you won't quit no matter how difficult the way might seem.

Lastly, you will require endurance. This is not an easy item to pack. You must purpose in your heart and mind that even though there may be hardship and stress you will hold onto everything God gives you to endure the process and that you will let go of those things that might hinder your progress. Sometimes you may fall, but you will stand again, for our Lord has a love that will not let you go.

Remember to first count the cost, then resolve to finish. Take courage from Him who preceded you in this way of distress and commit your heart, soul, mind, body, strength, and material resources to help overcome the ongoing effects of your past abuse. Take hold of the support our Lord offers you along the way and persevere during the dry times when you feel you cannot take one more step. Finally, walk this healing road with endurance as you remember His steps up a hill called Calvary and the price He paid that we might one day know freedom.

The grave could not hold Him back. The grave of your abuse will loose its hold on your life as well. In the course of your journey, you, too, will come to know power over death, the kind of emotional death that has robbed you in the past of joy, hope, and peace.

The following Scriptures are special ones that have ministered to the hearts of other survivors before you. May they bless you with added comfort and keep you strong and courageous for the journey. (For a discussion of ways to use the Scripture references, please see the Appendix.)

Cost

"For which one of you, when he wants to build a tower, does not first sit down and calculate the cost, to see if he has enough to complete it? Otherwise, when he has laid a foundation, and is not able to finish, all who observe it begin to ridicule him, saying, 'This man began to build and was not able to finish.' " *Luke 14:28-30*

Many therefore of His disciples, when they heard *this* said, "This is a difficult statement; who can listen to it?" . . . As a result of this many of His disciples withdrew, and were not walking with Him anymore. *John 6:60, 66*

Now the Lord said to Abram, "Go forth from your country, and from your relatives And from your father's house, To the land which I will show you; . . . ." *Genesis 12:1*

By faith Moses, when he had grown up, refused to be called the son of Pharaoh's daughter; choosing rather to endure ill-treatment with the people of God, than to enjoy the passing pleasures of sin; considering the reproach of Christ greater riches than the treasures of Egypt; for he was looking to the reward. *Hebrews 11:24-26*

Beloved, do not be surprised at the fiery ordeal among you, which comes upon you from your testing, as though some strange thing were happening to you; but to the degree that you share the sufferings of Christ, keep on rejoicing; so that also at the revelation of His glory, you may rejoice with exultation. If you are reviled for the name of Christ, you are blessed, because the Spirit of glory and of God rests with you.

1 Peter 4:12-14

And because of the surpassing greatness of the revelations, for this reason, to keep me from exalting myself, there was given me a thorn in the flesh, a messenger of Satan to buffet me — to keep me from exalting myself! Concerning this I entreated the Lord three times that it might depart from me. And He has said to me, "My grace is sufficient for you, for power is perfected in weakness." Most gladly, therefore, I will rather boast about my weaknesses, that the power of Christ may dwell in me. Therefore I am well content with weaknesses, with insults, with distresses, with persecutions, with difficulties, for Christ's sake; for when I am weak, then I am strong.   *2 Corinthians 12:7-10*

When you pass through the waters, I will be with you; And through the rivers, they will not overflow you. When you walk through the fire, you will not be scorched, Nor will the flame burn you.   *Isaiah 42:2*

. . . we are afflicted in every way, but not crushed; perplexed, but not despairing; persecuted, but not forsaken; struck down, but not destroyed;   *2 Corinthians 4:8-9*

"And everyone who has left houses or brothers or sisters or father or mother or children or farms for My name's sake, shall receive many times as much, and shall inherit eternal life."   *Matthew 19:29*

However, the king said to Araunah, "No, but I will surely buy it from you for a price, for I will not offer burnt offerings to the Lord my God which cost me nothing."   *2 Samuel 24:24*

Resolve

For the Lord God helps Me, Therefore, I am not disgraced; Therefore, I have set My face like flint, And I know that I shall not be ashamed.

Isaiah 50:7

By faith Abraham, when he was called, obeyed by going out to a place which he was to receive for an inheritance; and he went out, not knowing where he was going. *Hebrews 11:8*

Finally, brethren, whatever is true, whatever is honorable, whatever is right, whatever is pure, whatever is lovely, whatever is of good repute, if there is any excellence and if anything worthy of praise, let your mind dwell on these things. *Philippians 4:8*

So I answered them and said to them, "The God of heaven will give us success; therefore we His servants will arise and build, but you have no portion, right or memorial in Jerusalem." *Nehemiah 2:20*

So we built the wall and the whole wall was joined together to half its height, for the people had a mind to work. *Nehemiah 4:6*

For I am confident of this very thing, that He who began a good work in you will perfect it until the day of Christ Jesus. *Philippians 1:6*

And He is before all things, and in Him all things hold together.

Colossians 1:17

. . . for I know whom I have believed in and I am convinced that He is able to guard what I have entrusted to Him until that day.

2 Timothy 1:12

The human mind plans the way, but the Lord directs the steps.

Proverbs 16:9 (NRSV)

The human mind may devise many plans, but it is the purpose of the Lord that will be established.   *Proverbs 19:21* (NRSV)

Courage

Have I not commanded you? Be strong and courageous! Do not tremble or be dismayed, for the Lord your God is with you wherever you go.

Joshua 1:9

Now to Him who is able to do exceeding abundantly beyond all that we ask or think, according to the power that works within us, ...

Ephesians 3:20

Finally, be strong in the Lord, and in the strength of His might.

Ephesians 6:10

And they overcame him because of the blood of the Lamb and because of the word of their testimony, and they did not love their life even to death.   *Revelation 12:11*

The Lord will give strength to His people; The Lord will bless His people with peace.   *Psalm 29:11*

Be strong, and let your heart take courage, All you who hope in the Lord.   *Psalm 31:24*

Wait for the Lord; Be strong, and let your heart take courage; Yes, wait for the Lord.   *Psalm 27:14*

The wicked flee when no one is pursuing, But the righteous are bold as a lion.   *Proverbs 28:1*

What then shall we say to these things? If God is for us, who is against us?   *Romans 8:31*

For God has not given us a spirit of timidity, but of power and love and discipline.   *2 Timothy 1:7*

. . . Do not be afraid of them; remember the Lord who is great and awesome, and fight for your brothers, your sons, your daughters, your wives, and your houses.   *Nehemiah 4:14*

Be strong and courageous, do not be afraid or tremble at them for the Lord your God is the one who goes with you. He will not fail you or forsake you.   *Deuteronomy 31:6*

But you, be strong and do not lose courage, for there is reward for your work.   *2 Chronicles 15:7*

"These things I have spoken to you, that in Me you may have peace. In the world you have tribulation, but take courage; I have overcome the world."   *John 16:33*

". . . Take courage, My son, your sins are forgiven."   *Matthew 9:2*

". . . Daughter, take courage; your faith has made you well."
Matthew 9:22

". . . Take courage; for as you have solemnly witnessed to My cause at Jerusalem, so you must witness at Rome also."   *Acts 23:11*

Let us therefore draw near with confidence to the throne of grace, that we may receive mercy and may find grace to help in time of need.

Hebrews 4:16

You are from God, little children, and have overcome them; because greater is He who is in you than he who is in the world.   *1 John 4:4*

Commitment

Trust in the Lord with all your heart, And do not lean on your own understanding. In all your ways acknowledge Him, And He will make your paths straight.   *Proverbs 3:5-6*

Commit your way to the Lord, Trust also in Him, and He will do it. And He will bring forth your righteousness as the light, And your judgment as the noonday.   *Psalm 37:5-6*

Therefore, since we have so great a cloud of witnesses surrounding us, let us also lay aside every encumbrance, and the sin which so easily entangles us, and let us run with endurance the race that is set before us, fixing our eyes on Jesus, the author and perfecter of faith, who for the joy set before Him endured the cross, despising the shame, and has sat down at the right hand of the throne of God. For consider Him who has endured such hostility by sinners against Himself, so that you may not grow weary and lose heart.   *Hebrews 12:1-3*

Is this not the fast which I chose, To loosen the bonds of wickedness, To undo the bands of the yoke, And to let the oppressed go free, And break every yoke?   *Isaiah 58:6-7*

If it be so, our God whom we serve is able to deliver us from the furnace of blazing fire; and He will deliver us out of your hand, O king. But even if He does not, let it be known to you, O king, that we are not going to serve your gods or worship the golden image that you have set up.

Daniel 3:17-18

Therefore, let those also who suffer according to the will of God entrust their souls to a faithful Creator in doing what is right.   *1 Peter 4:19*

Commit your works to the Lord, And your plans will be established.
Proverbs 16:3

Finally, be strong in the Lord, and in the strength of His might. Put on the full armor of God, that you may be able to stand firm against the schemes of the devil.   *Ephesians 6:10-11*

I appeal to you therefore, brothers and sisters, by the mercies of God, to present your bodies as a living sacrifice, holy and acceptable to God, which is your spiritual worship. Do not be conformed to this world, but be transformed by the renewing of your minds, so that you may discern what is the will of God — what is good and acceptable and perfect.
Romans 12:1-2 (NRSV)

Therefore I run in such a way, as not without aim; I box in such a way as not beating the air; but I buffet my body and make it my slave, lest possible, after I have preached to others, I myself should be disqualified.
1 Corinthians 9:26-27

Or do you not know that your body is a temple of the Holy Spirit who is in you, whom you have from God, and that you are not your own? For you have been bought for a price: therefore glorify God in your body.
1 Corinthians 9:24-25

But as for me, I would seek God, And I would place my cause before God . . . .   *Job 5:8*

Support

"Do not fear, for I have redeemed you; I have called you by name; you are Mine!"   *Isaiah 43:1b*

Bear one another's burdens, and thus fulfill the law of Christ.

Galatians 6:2

"For the eyes of the Lord move to and fro throughout the earth that He may strongly support those whose heart is completely His. You have acted foolishly in this. Indeed, from now on you will surely have wars."

2 Chronicles 16:9

The Lord will accomplish what concerns me . . . .   *Psalm 138:8*

Then, the Lord knows how to rescue the godly from temptation, and to keep the unrighteous under punishment for the day of judgment.

2 Peter 2:9

And I will ask the Father, and He will give you another Helper, that He may be with you forever;   *John 14:16*

I will not leave you as orphans; I will come to you.   *John 14:18*

For the Lord will not abandon His people on account of His great name, because the Lord has been pleased to make you a people for Himself.

1 Samuel 12:22

Those who love me, I will deliver; I will protect those who know my name. When they call to me, I will answer them; I will be with them in trouble, I will rescue them and honor them.   *Psalm 91:14-15* (NRSV)

"Do not fear, for I am with you; do not anxiously look about you, for I am your God. I will strengthen you, surely I will help you, Surely I will uphold you with My righteous right hand."   *Isaiah 41:10*

"The afflicted and needy are seeking water, but there is none, And their tongue is parched with thirst; I, the Lord, will answer them Myself, As the God of Israel I will not forsake them."   *Isaiah 41:17*

For they are well instructed; their God teaches them.

Isaiah 28:26 (NRSV)

Cast your burden upon the Lord, and He will sustain you; He will never allow the righteous to be shaken.   *Psalm 55:22*

"Come unto Me, all who are weary and heavy-laden, and I will give you rest. Take My yoke upon you, and learn of Me, for I am gentle and humble in heart; and YOU SHALL FIND REST FOR YOUR SOULS. For My yoke is easy, and My load is light."   *Matthew 11:28-29*

"In My Father's house are many dwelling places; if it were not so, I would have told you; for I go to prepare a place for you. And if I go and prepare a place for you, I will come again, and receive you to Myself; that where I am, there you may be also."   *John 14:2-3*

So the wall was completed on the twenty-fifth of the month Elul, in fifty-two days. And it came about when all our enemies heard of it, and all the nations surrounding us saw it, they lost their confidence; for they recognized that this work had been accomplished with the help of our God.

Nehemiah 6:15-16

And He has said to me, "My grace is sufficient for you, for power is perfected in weakness." Most gladly, therefore, I will rather boast about my weaknesses, that the power of Christ may dwell in me.

2 Corinthians 12:9

Perseverance

For we through the Spirit, by faith, are waiting for the hope of righteousness.   *Galatians 5:4*

But if we hope for what we do not see, with perseverance we wait eagerly for it.   *Romans 8:25*

"You were tired out by the length of your road, Yet you did not say, 'It is hopeless.' You found renewed strength, Therefore you did not faint."
Isaiah 57:10

. . . for whatever is born of God conquers the world. And this is the victory that conquers the world, our faith. Who is it that conquers the world but the one who believes that Jesus is the Son of God?   *1 John 5:4, 5*

And after you have suffered for a little while, the God of all grace, who called you to His eternal glory in Christ, will Himself perfect, confirm, strengthen and establish you.   *1 Peter 5:10*

And they overcame him because of the blood of the Lamb and because of the word of their testimony, and they did not love their life even to death.   *Revelation 12:11*

With all prayer and petition pray at all times in the Spirit, and with this in view, be on the alert with all perseverance and petition for all the saints.
Ephesians 6:18

"Abide in me as I abide in you. Just as the branch cannot bear fruit by itself unless it abides in the vine, neither can you unless you abide in me. I am the vine, you are the branches. Those who abide in me, and I in them bear much fruit; because apart from me you can do nothing."
John 15:4-5 (NRSV)

Resist him, steadfast in your faith, for you know that your brothers and sisters in all the world are undergoing the same kinds of suffering.
1 Peter 5:9 (NRSV)

. . . but we also exult in our tribulations, knowing that tribulation brings about perseverance; and perseverance, proven character; and proven character, hope and hope does not disappoint . . . .   *Romans 5:3-5*

For whatever was written in earlier times was written for our instruction, that through perseverance and the encouragement of the Scriptures we might have hope. Now may the God who gives perseverance and encouragement grant you to be of the same mind . . . .   *Romans 15:4-5*

Rejoicing in hope, persevering in tribulation, devoted to prayer.
Romans 12:12

"And the *seed* in the good soil, these are the ones who have heard the word in an honest and good heart, and hold it fast, and bear fruit with perseverance."   *Luke 8:15*

Therefore, we ourselves speak proudly of you among the churches of God for your perseverance and faith in the midst of all your persecutions and afflictions which you endure.   *2 Thessalonians 1:4*

But flee from these things, you man of God; and pursue righteousness, godliness, faith, love, perseverance *and* gentleness.   *1 Timothy 6:11*

Now for this very reason also, applying all diligence, in your faith supply moral excellence, and in *your* moral excellence, knowledge; and in *your* knowledge, self-control, and in *your* self-control, perseverance, and in *your* perseverance, godliness;   *2 Peter 1:5-6*

Endurance

Therefore, since we have so great a cloud of witnesses surrounding us, let us also lay aside every encumbrance, and the sin which so easily entangles us, and let us run with endurance the race that is set before us, fixing our eyes on Jesus, the author and perfecter of faith, who for the joy set before Him endured the cross, despising the shame, and has sat down at the right hand of the throne of God. For consider Him who has endured such hostility by sinners against Himself, so that you may grow weary and lose heart.   *Hebrews 12:1-3*

Do you not know? Have you not heard? The Everlasting God, the Lord, the creator of the ends of the earth Does not become weary or tired. His understanding is inscrutable. He gives strength to the weary, And to him who lacks might he increases power.   *Isaiah 40:28-29*

And let endurance have its perfect result, that you may be perfect and complete, lacking in nothing.   *James 1:4*

Behold, we count those blessed who endured. You have heard of the endurance of Job and have seen the outcome of the Lord's dealings, that the Lord is full of compassion and is merciful.   *James 5:11*

Therefore, do not throw away your confidence, which has a great reward. For you have need of endurance, so that when you have done the will of God, you may receive what was promised.   *Hebrews 10:35-36*

Blessed is anyone who endures temptation. Such a one has stood the test and will receive the crown of life that the Lord has promised to those who love him.   *James 1:12* (NRSV)

And in a similar way these are the ones on whom seed was sown on the rocky places, who, when they hear the word, immediately receive it with joy; and they have no firm root in themselves, but are only temporary; then, when affliction or persecution arises because of the word, immediately they fall away.   *Mark 4:16-17*

But you, be sober in all things, endure hardship, do the work of an evangelist, fulfill your ministry.   *2 Timothy 4:5*

Can your heart endure, or can your hands be strong, in the days that I shall deal with you? I, the Lord, have spoken and shall act.

Ezekiel 22:14

Therefore, we ourselves speak proudly of you among the churches of God for your perseverance and faith in the midst of all your persecutions and afflictions which you endure.   *2 Thessalonians 1:4*

. . . what persecutions I endured, and out of them all the Lord delivered me! And indeed, all who desire to live godly in Christ Jesus will be persecuted.   *2 Timothy 3:11-12*

No testing has overtaken you that is not common to everyone. God is faithful, and he will not let you be tested beyond your strength, but with the testing he will also provide the way out so that you may be able to endure it.   *1 Corinthians 10:13* (NRSV)

Therefore, take up the full armor of God, that you may be able to resist in the evil day, and have done everything, to stand firm.

Ephesians 6:13

HEALING **JOURNAL**
leg 1 / cost

Use this page to record your personal thoughts and reflections.

leg 1 / cost

Use this page to record your special Bible verses that encourage you on the journey (verses need not be limited to the ones in this book).

HEALING **JOURNAL**
leg 2 / resolve

Use this page to record your personal thoughts and reflections.

leg 2 / resolve

Use this page to record your special Bible verses that encourage you on the journey (verses need not be limited to the ones in this book).

HEALING **JOURNAL**
leg 3 / courage

Use this page to record your personal thoughts and reflections.

leg 3 / courage

Use this page to record your special Bible verses that encourage you on the journey (verses need not be limited to the ones in this book).

HEALING **JOURNAL**
leg 4 / commitment

Use this page to record your personal thoughts and reflections.

leg 4 / commitment

Use this page to record your special Bible verses that encourage you on the journey (verses need not be limited to the ones in this book).

HEALING **JOURNAL**
leg 5 / support

Use this page to record your personal thoughts and reflections.

leg 5 / support

Use this page to record your special Bible verses that encourage you on the journey (verses need not be limited to the ones in this book).

HEALING **JOURNAL**
leg 6 / perseverance

Use this page to record your personal thoughts and reflections.

leg 6 / perseverance

Use this page to record your special Bible verses that encourage you on the journey (verses need not be limited to the ones in this book).

HEALING **JOURNAL**
leg 7 / endurance

Use this page to record your personal thoughts and reflections.

leg 7 / endurance

Use this page to record your special Bible verses that encourage you on the journey (verses need not be limited to the ones in this book).

2
PROVISIONS

On any journey there are personal needs that must be met. If you were thinking of taking an actual trip, you would require certain provisions to help you brave the voyage and overcome any obstacles along the way. For instance, you would want a safe place to sleep at night, protective covering in times of bad weather, food when you are hungry, water when you are thirsty, and a restroom when the need arises.

If you are to meet each challenge on the road to *recovery*, first you must have hope. Hope is believing that something you cannot yet see may truly come to pass. The end of your healing process from past abuse cannot be seen at the beginning, but hope tells you completion is possible.

How can you begin a trip if you have no hope whatsoever of completing it? *Hope, then, is not a luxury, it is an essential.*

Faith closely follows hope. Hebrews 11:1 explains that faith is the substance (assurance, or trust) of things hoped for, the evidence of things not seen. You can understand that such faith is indispensable when the road is difficult and the end is not in sight. The gift of faith will grow in your heart when you draw from His promises. As you see *His faithfulness to you* during the healing process, *your own faith* will grow and steadily be strengthened.

While looking at distortions from the past, honesty will be a light that shines into the dark places. When you are open and frank with yourself, the unknown can be transformed into clear sight and understanding. Are you ready to face the reality of what may have happened long ago? Can you let the memories surface without trying to minimize their effects on you? Honesty with oneself is a major part of personal recovery. Are you ready to seek truth in your life and face it openly?

To face deep personal pain from the past, you must find safety. When you experienced early abuse, you found there was no place to run, perhaps no safe person to tell, and often no safe feeling with which to respond. Now you are ready for a new step of growth.

Our Lord longs to provide the safety you need to face honestly what has occurred. When it seems that no safe corner can be found in this world, you will begin to discover the greatest safety of all, the safety of His everlasting arms (Deuteronomy 33:27b). In the most painful steps of your journey, feeling the presence of these arms may seem almost impossible. Thankfully, this emptiness doesn't remain forever, and the dawn of His presence at last begins to dissolve your struggle and grief.

Don't underestimate your need for safety, whether emotional or spiritual. Such growing security makes it possible to continue the journey without stopping short of your destination.

Stress must also be considered as one travels the road to wholeness, and relief cannot be overlooked. There will be times when everything feels out of control, times when you don't want to feel at all, times when anxious thoughts multiply within you. These are the moments when relief must be found. Deliverance from distress — genuine release — will come through understanding friends, through God's Word, and through learning to rethink who you are. Our society promotes different types of relief, but they keep you from facing inner turmoil. Various forms of addiction, such as the ones discussed in the next chapter, simply compound existing problems and leave you with a damaged sense of self-worth and seriously strained relationships.

Your identity is not marred or destroyed by the abuse you received, but the emotional tapes playing in your mind would convince you otherwise. The answer will not be found in eating, drinking, spending, and so on.

Every traveler has an important part to play in the area of relief. Part of your role is to be willing to learn to reach for the tools to ease stress or anxiety before it becomes overwhelming. A number of provisions are listed here. Use them. Your life need not be out of control for restoration to take place.

The move toward recovery will also involve openness. Do you want to be open to all God desires to reveal? Are you willing, if necessary, to let someone help you in time of need? Can you be open and humble enough to permit the feelings to come?

If you are closed to any or all of these aspects of being vulnerable, the pathway to healing could become more and more narrow. Ultimately, you may not be able to traverse it at all. Openness is not just an option for those who want to be free — it is a vital necessity. The time has passed for pretending; now is the time to open your heart to truth and reality.

These steps are not easy ones. Thankfully, the provisions needed and given do not stop there. Our Lord adds His own special comfort. He will bring people into your life who will reflect His love for you when you feel you can't or don't want to come to Him.

Little things will happen to remind you once again that He is there and will not leave you. When you don't think you can make it one more step of the way, He will bring His Word to your heart and gradually peace will begin to replace panic. Hope will begin to erase despair and the sense that somehow you are loved can break through the darkness of yesterday and the pain of today. The journey to recovery is worth the risk, for the God of all comfort will meet you at the point of your greatest need.

America has not traditionally been a nation that encourages its people to have or express emotions. How wonderful life would be if you didn't have to deal with those unpleasant things called feelings. Or would it?

Someone whose emotions have been damaged or shut down often cannot feel pain or sorrow, anger or despair. But, at the same time, such woundedness also robs an individual of pleasant feelings such as joy and happiness, sensitivity and tenderness, and even mercy and love.

One of the most important provisions for your path to emotional health will be permission to feel. This is not just God's permission for you to experience and release all the buried feelings, but your own permission as well.

Many people with repressed emotions have made a vow in childhood to never again be hurt so badly, even if it meant they would never again allow themselves to feel. Have you made such an inner promise? Perhaps it protected you at the time, but now is the season for healing in your life. Unhealthy vows must be broken and permission given to feel once again.

You will find that our Lord gives you that permission to feel, for He is a feeling God who walked this earth as a feeling man. He created you in His image, to have healthy emotions. Can you give yourself permission to express them in your life?

The Scriptures that follow convey His desire for you and His provisions of hope, faith, honesty, safety, relief, openness, comfort, and permission to feel. You will find these words to be a treasure of love and concern as you travel the path to wholeness. May they be a blessing to you even as they have blessed many fellow travelers before you on the way.

Hope

For whatever was written in earlier times was written for our instruction, that through perseverance and the encouragement of the Scriptures we might have hope.   *Romans 15:4*

And not only this, but we also exult in our tribulations, knowing that tribulation brings about perseverance; and perseverance, proven character; and proven character, hope; and hope does not disappoint because the love of God has been poured out within our hearts through the Holy Spirit who was given to us.   *Romans 5:5*

Now faith is the assurance of things hoped for, the conviction of things not seen.   *Hebrews 11:1*

And He is before all things, and in Him all things hold together;
Colossians 1:17

For our citizenship is in heaven, from which also we eagerly wait for a Savior, the Lord Jesus Christ;   *Philippians 3:20*

And He shall wipe away every tear from their eyes; and there shall no longer be any death; there shall no longer be any mourning, or crying, or pain; the first things have passed away.   *Revelation 21:4*

In thy lovingkindness Thou hast led the people whom Thou hast redeemed; In Thy strength Thou hast guided them to Thy holy habitation.

Exodus 15:13

Hope deferred makes the heart sick, But desire fulfilled is a tree of life.

Proverbs 13:12

But now, thus says the Lord, your creator, O Jacob, And he who formed you, O Israel, "Do not fear, for I have redeemed you; I have called you by name; you are Mine! When you pass through the waters, I will be with you; And through the rivers, they will not overflow you. When you walk through the fire, you will not be scorched, Nor will the flame burn you. for I am the Lord your God, The Holy One of Israel, your Savior"; . . . .

Isaiah 43:1-3

For thus says the high and exalted One Who lives forever, whose name is Holy, "I dwell on a high and holy place, And also with the contrite and lowly of spirit In order to revive the spirit of the lowly And to revive the heart of the contrite."   *Isaiah 57:15*

He will send from heaven and save me, he will put to shame those who trample on me. God will send forth his steadfast love and his faithfulness.   *Psalm 57:3* (NRSV)

For Thy righteousness, O God, reaches to the heavens, Thou who hast done great things; O God who is like thee? Thou, who hast shown me many troubles and distresses, Wilt revive me again, And wilt bring me up again from the depths of the earth. Mayest Thou increase my greatness, And turn to comfort me.   *Psalm 71:19-21*

Blessed be the God and Father of our Lord Jesus Christ, who according to His great mercy has caused us to be born again to a living hope through the resurrection of Jesus Christ from the dead, to obtain an inheritance which is imperishable and undefiled and will not fade away, reserved in heaven for you.   *1 Peter 1:3*

But since we are of the day, let us be sober, having put on the breastplate of faith and love, and as a helmet, the hope of salvation.
1 Thessalonians 5:8

[Love] bears all things, believes all things, hopes all things, endures all things. *1 Corinthians 13:7*

I would have despaired unless I had believed that I would see the goodness of the Lord In the land of the living. Wait for the Lord; Be strong, and let your heart take courage; Yes, wait for the Lord.
Psalm 27:13-14

The Lord will give strength to His people; The Lord will bless His people with peace. *Psalm 29:11*

And do not take the word of truth utterly out of my mouth, For I have hoped in Thine ordinances. *Psalm 119:43*

May those who fear Thee see me and be glad, Because I hope in Thy word. *Psalm 119:74*

I pray that the eyes of your heart may be enlightened, so that you may know what is the hope of His calling, what are the riches of the glory of His inheritance in the saints. *Ephesians 1:18*

. . . for the creation was subjected to futility, not of its own will but because of Him who subjected it, in hope that the creation itself will be set free from its bondage to decay and will obtain the freedom of the glory of the children of God. We know that the whole creation has been groaning in labor pains until now; and not only the creation, but we ourselves, who have the first fruits of the Spirit, groan inwardly while we wait for adoption, the redemption of our bodies. For in hope we were saved. Now hope that is seen is not hope. For who hopes for what is seen? But if we hope for what we do not see, we wait for it with patience.
Romans 8:20-25 (NRSV)

But as for me, I will hope continually, And will praise Thee yet more and more.   *Psalm 71:14*

Why are you in despair, O my soul? And why are you disturbed within me? Hope in God for I shall again praise Him, The help of my countenance, and my God.   *Psalm 43:5*

Now may the God of hope fill you with all joy and peace in believing, that you may abound in hope by the power of the Holy Spirit.
Romans 15:13

The human mind plans the way, but the Lord directs the steps.
Proverbs 16:9 (NRSV)

Be assured, the wicked will not go unpunished, but those who are righteous will escape.   *Proverbs 11:21* (NRSV)

Do not be afraid of sudden fear, Nor of the onslaught of the wicked when it comes; For the Lord will be your confidence, And will keep your foot from being caught.   *Proverbs 3:25-26*

The Lord will accomplish what concerns me; . . . .   *Psalm 138:8a*

Even to your old age, I shall be the same, And even to your graying years I shall bear you! I have done it, and I shall carry you; And I shall bear you, and I shall deliver you.   *Isaiah 46:4*

Faith

Then Job answered the Lord, and said, "I know that Thou canst do all things, And that no purpose of Thine can be thwarted."   *Job 42:1-2*

Look at the proud! Their spirit is not right in them, but the righteous by their faith.   *Habakkuk 2:4* (NRSV)

For whatever is born of God conquers the world. And this is the victory that conquers the world, our faith. Who is it that conquers the world but the one who believes that Jesus is the Son of God.   *1 John 5:4-5* (NRSV)

In this you greatly rejoice, even though now for a little while, if necessary, you have been distressed by various trials, that the proof of your faith, being more precious than gold which is perishable, even though tested by fire, may be found to result in praise and glory and honor at the revelation of Jesus Christ;   *1 Peter 1:7*

. . . knowing that the testing of your faith produces endurance. And let endurance have its perfect result, that you may be perfect and complete, lacking in nothing.   *James 1:3*

And without faith it is impossible to please God, for whoever would approach him must believe that he exists and that he rewards those who seek him.   *Hebrews 11:6* (NRSV)

Therefore, since we have so great a cloud of witnesses surrounding us, let us also lay aside every encumbrance, and the sin which so easily entangles us, and let us run with endurance the race that is set before us, fixing our eyes on Jesus, the author and perfecter of faith, ...   *Hebrews 12:1*

And what more shall I say? For time will fail me if I tell of Gideon, Barak, Samson, Jephthah, of David and Samuel and the prophets, who by faith conquered kingdoms, performed acts of righteousness, obtained promises, shut the mouths of lions, quenched the power of fire, escaped the edge of the sword, from weakness were made strong, because mighty in war, put foreign armies to flight.   *Hebrews 11:33-34*

Let us hold fast the confession of our hope without wavering, for He who promised is faithful;   *Hebrews 10:23*

For by grace you have been saved through faith; and that not of yourselves, it is the gift of God;   *Ephesians 2:8*

. . . for we walk by faith, not by sight . . . .   *2 Corinthians 5:4*

Our steps are made firm by the Lord, when he delights in our way;
though we stumble, we shall not fall headlong, for the Lord holds us by
the hand.   *Psalm 37:23-24* (NRSV)

But as for me, I trust in Thee, O Lord, I say, Thou art my God. My times
are in Thy hand; Deliver me from the hand of my enemies, and from
those who persecute me.   *Psalm 31:14-15*

And the Lord said, "If you had faith like a mustard seed, you would say
to this mulberry tree, 'Be uprooted and be planted in the sea'; and it
would obey you."   *Luke 17:6*

Know therefore that the Lord your God, He is God, the faithful God,
who keeps His covenant and His lovingkindness to a thousandth generation with those who love Him and keep His commandments;
Deuteronomy 7:9

O love the Lord, all you His godly ones! The Lord preserves the faithful,
And fully recompenses the proud doer.   *Psalm 31:23*

By faith even Sarah herself received ability to conceive, even beyond the
proper time of life, since she considered Him faithful who had promised;
Hebrews 11:11

But the Lord is faithful, and He will strengthen and protect you from the
evil one.   *2 Thessalonians 3:3*

Faithful is He who calls you, and He also will bring it to pass.
2 Thessalonians 5:24

But if God so clothes the grass of the field, which is alive today and tomorrow is thrown into the oven, how much more will he clothe you — you of little faith!   *Luke 12:28* (NRSV)

Now faith is the assurance of things hoped for, the conviction of things not seen.   *Hebrews 11:1*

Honesty

"Only fear the Lord and serve Him in truth with all your heart; for consider what great things He has done for you."   *Isaiah 12:24*

O Lord, who may abide in your tent? Who may dwell on your holy hill? Those who walk blamelessly, and do what is right, and speak the truth from their heart; . . . .   *Psalm 15:1-2* (NRSV)

Lead me in Thy truth and teach me, For Thou art the God of my salvation; For Thee I wait all the day.   *Psalm 25:5*

Into Thy hand I commit my spirit; Thou hast ransomed me, O Lord, God of truth.   *Psalm 31:5*

Behold, Thou dost desire truth in the innermost being, And in the hidden part Thou wilt make me know wisdom.   *Psalm 51:6*

Thou hast given a banner to those who fear Thee, That it may be displayed because of the truth.   *Psalm 60:4*

Teach me Thy way, O Lord; I will walk in Thy truth; . . . . *Psalm 86:11*

But Thou, O Lord, art a God merciful and gracious, Slow to anger and abundant in lovingkindness and truth. *Psalm 86:15*

The Lord is near to all who call upon Him, To all who call upon Him in truth. *Psalm 145:18*

Do not let kindness and truth leave you; Bind them around your neck, Write them on the tablet of your heart. *Proverbs 3:3*

Whoever speaks truth gives honest evidence, but a false witness speaks deceitfully. *Proverbs 12:17* (NRSV)

By lovingkindness and truth iniquity is atoned for, And by the fear of the Lord one keeps away from evil. *Proverbs 16:6*

A false witness will perish, But the man who listens *to the truth* will speak forever. *Proverbs 21:28*

"Behold, I will bring to it health and healing, and I will heal them; and I will reveal to them an abundance of peace and truth." *Jeremiah 33:6*

"These are the things which you should do: speak the truth to one another; Judge with truth and judgment for peace in your gates."
Zechariah 8:16

But the woman fearing and trembling, aware of what had happened to her, came and fell down before Him, and told Him the whole truth.
Mark 5:33

And the Word became flesh, and dwelt among us, and we beheld His glory, glory as of the only begotten from the Father, full of grace and truth.   *John 1:14*

"God is spirit, and those who worship Him must worship in spirit and truth."   *John 4:24*

". . . and you shall know the truth, and the truth shall make you free."
John 8:32

Jesus said to him, "I am the way, and the truth, and the life; no one comes to the Father, but through Me."   *John 14:6*

Those who walk righteously and speak uprightly, who despise the gain of oppression, who wave away a bribe instead of accepting it, who stop their ears from hearing of bloodshed and shut their eyes from looking on evil, they will live on the heights; their refuge will be the fortresses of rocks; their food will be supplied, their water assured.
Isaiah 33:15-16 (NRSV)

"Sanctify them in the truth; Thy word is truth."   *John 17:17*

. . . does not rejoice in unrighteousness, but rejoices with the truth;
1 Corinthians 13:6

. . . but speaking the truth in love, we are to grow up in all *aspects* into Him, who is the head, *even* Christ.   *Ephesians 4:15*

Therefore, laying aside falsehood, speak truth, each one *of you,* with his neighbor, for we are members of one another.   *Ephesians 4:25*

Stand firm therefore, having girded your loins with truth, and having put on the breastplate of righteousness.   *Ephesians 6:14*

. . . who desires everyone to be saved and to come to the knowledge of the truth.   *1 Timothy 2:4* (NRSV)

. . . always learning and never able to come to the knowledge of truth.
2 Timothy 3:7

Do not withhold good from those to whom it is due, When it is in your power to do *it*.   *Proverbs 3:27*

Safety

Thou art my hiding place; Thou dost preserve me from trouble; Thou dost surround me with songs of deliverance.   *Psalm 32:7*

You who live in the shelter of the Most High, who abide in the shadow of the Almighty, will say to the Lord, "My refuge and my fortress; my God, in whom I trust!"   *Psalm 91:1-2* (NRSV)

"And also the Glory of Israel will not lie or change His mind; for He is not a man that He should change His mind."   *1 Samuel 15:29*

"No weapon that is formed against you shall prosper; And every tongue that accuses you in judgment you will condemn. This is the heritage of the servants of the Lord, And their vindication is from Me," declares the Lord.   *Isaiah 54:17*

Those who love me, I will deliver; I will protect those who know my name. When they call to me, I will answer them; I will be with them in trouble, I will rescue them and honor them.   *Psalm 91:14-15* (NRSV)

"Listen to Me, O house of Jacob, And all the remnant of the house of Israel, You who have been borne by Me from birth, And have been carried from the womb; Even to your old age, I shall be the same, And even to your graying years I shall bear *you!* I have done *it,* and I shall carry *you;* And I shall bear *you,* and I shall deliver *you.*   *Isaiah 46:3-4*

God is in the midst of the city, it shall not be moved; God will help it when the morning dawns.   *Psalm 46:5* (NRSV)

"Peace I leave with you; My peace I give to you; not as the world gives, do I give to you. Let not your heart be troubled, nor let it be fearful."
John 14:27

Even though I walk through the valley of the shadow of death, I fear no evil; for Thou art with me; Thy rod and Thy staff, they comfort me.
Psalm 23:4

So we can say with confidence, "The Lord is my helper; I will not be afraid. What can anyone do to me?"   *Hebrews 13:6* (NRSV)

He will cover you with His pinions, And under His wings you may seek refuge; His faithfulness is a shield and bulwark. You will not be afraid of the terror by night, Or of the arrow that flies by day; Of the pestilence that stalks in darkness, Or of the destruction that lays waste at noon. A thousand may fall at your side, And ten thousand at your right hand; *But* it shall not approach you.   *Psalm 91:4-7*

"When you pass through the waters, I will be with you; And through the rivers, they will not overflow you. When you walk through the fire, you will not be scorched, Nor will the flame burn you."   *Isaiah 43:2*

The fear of others lays a snare, but one who trusts in the Lord is secure.
Proverbs 29:25 (NRSV)

Do not be afraid of sudden fear, Nor of the onslaught of the wicked when it comes; For the Lord will be your confidence, And will keep your foot from being caught.   *Proverbs 3:25-26*

"The eternal God is a dwelling place, And underneath are the everlasting arms; And He drove out the enemy from before you, And said, 'Destroy!' "   *Deuteronomy 33:27*

So that He sets on high those who are lowly, And those who mourn are lifted to safety.   *Job 5:11*

In peace I will both lie down and sleep, For Thou alone, O Lord, dost make me to dwell in safety.   *Psalm 4:8*

"Because the poor are despoiled, because the needy groan, I will now rise up," says the Lord; "I will place them in the safety for which they long."
                                        Psalm 12:5 (NRSV)

The name of the Lord is a strong tower; The righteous runs into it and is safe.   *Proverbs 18:10*

When my anxious thoughts multiply within me, Thy consolations delight my soul.   *Psalm 94:19*

The Lord is your keeper; The Lord is your shade on your right hand. The sun will not smite you by day, Nor the moon by night. The Lord will protect you from all evil; He will keep your soul. The Lord will guard your going out and your coming in From this time forth and forever.
                                        Psalm 121:5-8

Relief

"I will feed My flock and I will lead them to rest," declares the Lord God.   *Ezekiel 34:15*

"Come to Me, all who are weary and heavy-laden, and I will give you rest."   *Matthew 11:28*

"Take My yoke upon you, and learn from Me, for I am gentle and humble in heart; and you shall find rest for your souls."   *Matthew 11:29*

He makes me lie down in green pastures; He leads me beside quiet waters. He restores my soul; He guides me in the paths of righteousness For His name's sake. Even though I walk through the valley of the shadow of death, I fear no evil; for Thou art with me; Thy rod and Thy staff, they comfort me.   *Psalm 23:2-4*

Blessed be the Lord, who daily bears our burden, The God *who* is our salvation.   *Psalm 68:19*

"The Lord your God is in your midst, A victorious warrior. He will exult over you with joy, He will be quiet in His love, He will rejoice over you with shouts of joy."   *Zephaniah 3:17*

When my anxious thoughts multiply within me, Thy consolations delight my soul.   *Psalm 94:19*

Many are the afflictions of the righteous, but the Lord rescues them from them all.   *Psalm 34:19* (NRSV)

The Lord is near to the brokenhearted, And saves those who are crushed in spirit.   *Psalm 34:18*

The Lord redeems the soul of His servants; And none of those who take refuge in Him will be condemned.   *Psalm 34:22*

. . . casting all your anxiety upon Him, because He cares for you.
1 Peter 5:7

Be anxious for nothing, but in everything by prayer and supplication with thanksgiving let your requests be made known to God. And the peace of God, which surpasses all comprehension, shall guard your hearts and your minds in Christ Jesus. Finally, brethren, whatever is true, whatever is honorable, whatever is right, whatever is pure, whatever is lovely, whatever is of good repute, if there is any excellence and if anything worthy of praise, let your mind dwell on these things.
Philippians 4:6-8

I will bless the Lord who has counseled me; Indeed, my mind instructs me in the night.   *Psalm 16:7*

Be still before the Lord, and wait patiently for him; do not fret over those who prosper in their way, over those who carry out evil devices.
Psalm 37:7 (NRSV)

Thou art my hiding place; Thou dost preserve me from trouble; Thou dost surround me with songs of deliverance.   *Psalm 32:7*

The Lord will command His lovingkindness in the daytime; And His song will be with me in the night, A prayer to the God of my life.
Psalm 42:8

"My sheep hear My voice, and I know them, and they follow Me; and I give eternal life to them, and they shall never perish; and no one shall snatch them out of My hand. My Father, who has given *them* to Me, is greater than all; and no one is able to snatch *them* out of the Father's hand."   *John 10:27-29*

Openness

"Call to Me, and I will answer you, and I will tell you great and mighty things, which you do not know."   *Jeremiah 33:3*

Let the words of my mouth and the meditation of my heart Be acceptable in Thy sight, O Lord, my rock and my Redeemer.   *Psalm 19:14*

Teach me to do Thy will, For Thou art my God; Let Thy good Spirit lead me on level ground. For the sake of Thy name, O Lord, revive me. In Thy righteousness bring my soul out of trouble.   *Psalm 143:10-11*

Restore to me the joy of Thy salvation, And sustain me with a willing spirit.   *Psalm 51:12*

Search me, O God, and know my heart; Try me and know my anxious thoughts; And see if there be any hurtful way in me, And lead me in the everlasting way.   *Psalm 139:23-24*

Behold, Thou dost desire truth in the innermost being, And in the hidden part Thou wilt make me know wisdom.   *Psalm 51:6*

"And you will seek Me and find *Me,* when you search for Me with all your heart."   *Jeremiah 29:13*

"As for you, my son Solomon, know the God of your father, and serve Him with a whole heart and a willing mind; for the Lord searches all hearts, and understands every intent of the thoughts."
                                    1 Chronicles 28:9a

"Keep watching and praying, that you may not enter into temptation; the spirit is willing, but the flesh is weak."   *Matthew 26:41*

The eyes of the Lord are toward the righteous, And His ears are *open* to their cry. *Psalm 34:15*

And there is no creature hidden from His sight, but all things are open and laid bare to the eyes of Him with whom we have to do.

Hebrews 4:13

Comfort

"Come to Me, all who are weary and heavy-laden, and I will give you rest. Take My yoke upon you, and learn from Me, for I am gentle and humble in heart; and you shall find rest for your souls. For My yoke is easy, and My load is light." *Matthew 11:28-30*

Let your character be free from the love of money, being content with what you have; for He Himself has said, "I will never desert you, nor will I ever forsake you." *Hebrews 13:5*

Go through, go through the gates; Clear the way for the people; Build up, build up the highway; Remove the stones, lift up a standard over the peoples. Behold, the Lord has proclaimed to the end of the earth, Say to the daughter of Zion, "Lo, your salvation comes; Behold His reward is with Him, and His recompense before Him." And they will call them, "The holy people, The redeemed of the Lord"; And you will be called, "Sought out, a city not forsaken." *Isaiah 62:10-12*

Even though I walk through the valley of the shadow of death, I fear no evil; for Thou art with me; Thy rod and Thy staff, they comfort me.

Psalm 23:4

This is my comfort in my affliction, That Thy word has revived me.

Psalm 119:50

"Then the virgin shall rejoice in the dance, And the young men and the old, together, For I will turn their mourning into joy, And will comfort them, and give them joy for their sorrow.   *Jeremiah 31:13*

Blessed *be* the God and Father of our Lord Jesus Christ, the Father of mercies and God of all comfort; who comforts us in all our affliction so that we may be able to comfort those who are in any affliction with the comfort with which we ourselves are comforted by God. For just as the sufferings of Christ are ours in abundance, so also our comfort is abundant through Christ.   *2 Corinthians 1:3-5*

The Lord is near to all who call upon Him, To all who call upon Him in truth.   *Psalm 145:18*

. . . For He gives to His beloved *even in his* sleep.   *Psalm 127:2*

Just as a father has compassion on *his* children, So the Lord has compassion on those who fear Him. For He Himself knows our frame; He is mindful that we are *but* dust.   *Psalm 103:13-14*

When my anxious thoughts multiply within me, Thy consolations delight my soul.   *Psalm 94:19*

For Thy righteousness, O God, *reaches* to the heavens, Thou who hast done great things; O God, who is like Thee? Thou, who hast shown me many troubles and distresses, Wilt revive me again, And wilt bring me up again from the depths of the earth. . . . And turn *to* comfort me.
Psalm 71:19-21

Thou hast taken account of my wanderings; Put my tears in Thy bottle; Are *they* not in Thy book?   *Psalm 56:8*

For my father and my mother have forsaken me, But the Lord will take me up.   *Psalm 27:10*

But now, thus says the Lord, your Creator, O Jacob, And He who formed you, O Israel, "Do not fear, for I have redeemed you; I have called you by name; you are Mine! When you pass through the waters, I will be with you; And through the rivers, they will not overflow you. When you walk through the fire, you will not be scorched, Nor will the flame burn you. For I am the Lord your God, The Holy One of Israel, your Savior; I have given Egypt as your ransom, Cush and Seba in your place. Since you are precious in My sight, *Since* you are honored and I love you, I will give *other* men in your place and *other* peoples in exchange for your life. Do not fear, for I am with you; I will bring your offspring from the east, And gather you from the west. I will say to the north, 'Give *them* up!' And to the south, 'Do not hold *them* back.' Bring My sons from afar, And My daughters from the ends of the earth, Everyone who is called by My name, And whom I have created for My glory, Whom I have formed, even whom I have made." *Isaiah 43:1-7*

"Fear not, for you will not be put to shame; Neither feel humiliated, for you will not be disgraced; But you will forget the shame of your youth, And the reproach of your widowhood you will remember no more. For your husband is your Maker, Whose name is the Lord of hosts; And your Redeemer is the Holy One of Israel, Who is called the God of all the earth. For the Lord has called you, Like a wife forsaken and grieved in spirit, Even like a wife of *one's* youth when she is rejected," Says your God. "For a brief moment I forsook you, But with great compassion I will gather you. In an outburst of anger I hid My face from you for a moment; But with everlasting lovingkindness I will have compassion on you," Says the Lord your Redeemer. *Isaiah 54:4-8*

Permission To Feel

There is an appointed time for everything. And there is a time for every event under heaven — A time to give birth, and a time to die; A time to plant, and a time to uproot what is planted. A time to kill, and a time to heal; A time to tear down, and a time to build up. A time to weep, and a time to laugh; A time to mourn, and a time to dance. A time to throw stones, and a time to gather stones; A time to embrace, and a time to shun embracing. A time to search, and a time to give up as lost; a time to keep, and a time to throw away. A time to tear apart, and a time to sew together; A time to be silent, and a time to speak. A time to love, and a time to hate; A time for war, and a time for peace.   *Ecclesiastes 3:1-8*

And about the ninth hour Jesus cried out with a loud voice, saying, "Eli, Eli, lama sabachthani?" that is, "My God, My God, why hast Thou forsaken Me?"   *Matthew 27:46*

Jesus wept.   *John 11:35*

Rejoice with those who rejoice, and weep with those who weep.
                                                                              Romans 12:15

Submit therefore to God. Resist the devil and he will flee from you. Draw near to God and He will draw near to you. Cleanse your hands, you sinners; and purify your hearts, you double-minded. Be miserable and mourn and weep; let your laughter be turned into mourning, and your joy to gloom. Humble yourselves in the presence of the Lord, and He will exalt you.   *James 4:7-10*

Since then we have a great high priest who has passed through the heavens, Jesus the Son of God, let us hold fast our confession. For we do not have a high priest who cannot sympathize with our weaknesses, but One who has been tempted in all things as *we are, yet* without sin. Let us therefore draw near with confidence to the throne of grace, that we may receive mercy and may find grace to help in time of need.
                                                                              Hebrews 4:14-16

From *my* distress I called upon the Lord; The Lord answered me *and set me* in a large place.   *Psalm 118:5*

Depart from me, all you who do iniquity, For the Lord has heard the voice of my weeping. The Lord has heard my supplication, The Lord receives my prayer.   *Psalm 6:8-9*

For His anger is but for a moment, His favor is for a lifetime; Weeping may last for the night, But a shout of joy *comes* in the morning.

Psalm 30:5

Be angry, and *yet* do not sin; do not let the sun go down on your anger, ... *Ephesians 4:26*

Rejoice with those who rejoice, and weep with those who weep.

Romans 12:15

"And you will say this word to them, 'Let my eyes flow down with tears night and day, And let them not cease; For the virgin daughter of my people has been crushed with a mighty blow, With a sorely infected wound." *Jeremiah 14:17*

May those who sow in tears reap with shouts of joy. Those who go out weeping, bearing the seed for sowing, shall come home with shouts of joy, carrying their sheaves. *Psalm 126:5-6* (NRSV)

I cry aloud with my voice to the Lord; I make supplication with my voice to the Lord. I pour out my complaint before Him; I declare my trouble before Him. When my spirit was overwhelmed within me, Thou didst know my path. In the way where I walk They have hidden a trap for me.

Psalm 142:1-3

Thou hast taken account of my wanderings; Put my tears in Thy bottle; Are *they* not in Thy book? *Psalm 56:8*

"Hear my prayer, O Lord, and give ear to my cry; do not hold your peace at my tears. For I am your passing guest, an alien, like all my forebears." *Psalm 39:12* (NRSV)

By the rivers of Babylon, There we sat down and wept, When we remembered Zion. Upon the willows in the midst of it We hung our harps.

Psalm 137:1-2

"Therefore, I will not restrain my mouth; I will speak in the anguish of my spirit, I will complain in the bitterness of my soul."   *Job 7:11*

"I loathe my own life; I will give full vent to my complaint; I will speak in the bitterness of my soul."   *Job 10:1*

HEALING **JOURNAL**
leg 8 / hope

Use this page to record your personal thoughts and reflections.

leg 8 / hope

Use this page to record your special Bible verses that encourage you on the
journey (verses need not be limited to the ones in this book).

HEALING **JOURNAL**
leg 9 / faith

Use this page to record your personal thoughts and reflections.

leg 9 / faith

Use this page to record your special Bible verses that encourage you on the journey (verses need not be limited to the ones in this book).

HEALING **JOURNAL**
leg 10 / honesty

Use this page to record your personal thoughts and reflections.

leg 10 / honesty

Use this page to record your special Bible verses that encourage you on the journey (verses need not be limited to the ones in this book).

HEALING **JOURNAL**
leg 11 / safety

Use this page to record your personal thoughts and reflections.

leg 11 / safety

Use this page to record your special Bible verses that encourage you on the journey (verses need not be limited to the ones in this book).

HEALING **JOURNAL**
leg 12 / relief

Use this page to record your personal thoughts and reflections.

leg 12 / relief

Use this page to record your special Bible verses that encourage you on the journey (verses need not be limited to the ones in this book).

HEALING **JOURNAL**
leg 13 / openness

Use this page to record your personal thoughts and reflections.

leg 13 / openness

Use this page to record your special Bible verses that encourage you on the journey (verses need not be limited to the ones in this book).

HEALING **JOURNAL**
leg 14 / comfort

Use this page to record your personal thoughts and reflections.

leg 14 / comfort

Use this page to record your special Bible verses that encourage you on the journey (verses need not be limited to the ones in this book).

HEALING **JOURNAL**
leg 15 / permission to feel

Use this page to record your personal thoughts and reflections.

leg 15 / permission to feel

Use this page to record your special Bible verses that encourage you on the journey (verses need not be limited to the ones in this book).

3
THE JOURNEY

One passage of Scripture that seems to confuse and immobilize many Christians today is the verse in which God calls Abraham to be perfect or to walk perfectly before Him. As spoken to Abraham, the Hebrew word *tamilym* or perfect translates "complete or whole." Jesus repeats the same type of command in the New Testament.

In Matthew 5:48 Jesus said, ". . . you are to be perfect [complete, whole], as your heavenly Father is perfect [complete, whole]." *To be complete is to become Christlike.* The journey toward wholeness is one that Christians are called to take. In the process of this adventure, you will begin to reflect Jesus, for He is truly whole.

You will pass through each of these areas before healing becomes a reality:

Denial / Shock
Anger
Release (betrayal; shame / doubt; guilt; loss / sadness)
Acceptance
Forgiveness

Sometimes the struggle involves two or more of these experienced concurrently, but each stands between the victim and victory over past abuse. While it may appear that some will pass through each step of the journey as they are listed, others may reexperience a number of stages as the truth becomes more real in their lives.

As you pass through denial and shock, you may not really believe all that has happened to you. You may hear yourself saying, "How could anyone have done such a thing to another human being? It can't be true. I must be making this up. I must be a terrible person to think such things." These are all normal responses. Virtually all survivors seem to have them in common.

Many people in denial run to and fro trying to fill their lives so they won't have to face the truth. Some become seriously codependent, taking care of everyone but themselves, while others may immerse themselves in such addictions as eating, fasting, spending, alcohol, gambling, and so on. How sad that the very truth that can set you free is often that from which you run away.

You don't always mean to hide from yourself, but sometimes you are so afraid that you make poor choices. You find it easier to deny what has happened to you than face the next struggle along the way of healing. Don't be surprised if denial and shock raise their heads more than once as you travel toward emotional health.

Perhaps you will find that you have been in denial for years and now the Lord is opening up the truth to your heart. Don't condemn yourself for not facing it earlier. The Lord has allowed that denial to protect and cushion your mind until such time as you are ready to face the road to freedom. Now you are ready to move beyond that fortress and reach for recovery.

Anger is another necessary step along the way. That little one of the memory, hurt so long ago, holds valid anger inside. The Lord desires you to pour out that anger in a safe and healthy way. He knows that it lives down deep inside you and He wants you to be free from it. Unfortunately, our fellow Christians have often made us feel that showing anger in any form is a sin. In truth, Scripture exhorts us to be angry but sin not (Ephesians 4:26). This verse would indicate that there is a healthy way to be angry. As you move through the legitimate anger you feel because of what happened to you, you will find this to be true.

The third phase of the journey, release, holds the key to many of your feelings. You will sense the shock and reality that an adult who should have protected you could actually abuse and cause you serious pain. If the abuser were a family member, or even if it were a stranger, there is a strong feeling of betrayal. Children are trusting and believe that adults are almost like God. Under the circumstances, to feel betrayed is a normal response.

There will be shame and doubt as you travel the road to restoration. If you have known abuse, the personal shame can be overwhelming almost to the point of destroying your self-image.

When you walk back through the roots of that shame, the insecurity can make you vulnerable and tender. It is a painful time but so essential to your recovery. Don't run from it. God will transform your shame, but first you must be willing to recognize and feel it.

False guilt is always attached to the violation committed against you. Because a child believes grownups to be virtually Godlike, anything bad that happens is somehow the child's fault. Thoughts such as "I must have done something horrible to make him treat me this way" or "I must be really bad if she thinks I deserve this" are natural and common. Even when the child is too young to think these thoughts, the responses are still there. You will be able to walk away from this false guilt as you examine what happened to you and allow yourself to feel the hurt you shut out as a child.

The loss of childhood is a sad occurrence. All the "what ifs" and "if onlys" are lodged deep in the heart of a victim. On the road to freedom you must face the genuine losses and allow yourself time to grieve over things you cannot go back and change. There will be times when you must also grieve over things you wanted that can never be. Only then can you move on to all the good things that *can* be and to the wonder of who you really are.

As you move out of the feelings of denial, shock, anger, and release, you will find a certain acceptance and calm beginning to emerge inside. You know that the abuse was real. You know it happened to you and it was horrible, but somehow *you have survived!* The raging storm is almost over, the winter is passing; spring is near and with it a new sense of anticipation that is infectious and overwhelming.

This last step of acceptance leads us into the most frequently misunderstood final phase of the journey. The area of forgiveness sets the teeth of many survivors on edge. It is as if the perpetrator will go free if they are forgiven. Who can make them pay? How will they ever know what they have done to you?

Some survivors confront the abuser; others feel it inappropriate to do so. Some perpetrators are deceased, some old and senile. To confront a victimizer is the choice of each survivor and should be prayerfully considered. *Only our Lord knows if it is right for you.* If the offender is still in a position to abuse other children, then you have a responsibility to do all you can to protect others as well as yourself. However, if this is not the case, seek the Lord for His heart in the matter and for His timing.

Remember that your forgiveness does not free the abuser; *it frees you.* Those who have committed the act(s) against you are now turned over to the God of all eternity. He has made the outcome very clear: "Vengeance is mine" (Hebrews 10:30); "It is a fearful thing to fall into the hands of the living God" (Hebrews 10:31).

Forgiveness can free your heart from bitterness and hatred when you are ready to put them away. It is important to understand that this type of forgiveness is not for those who are just recognizing the assaults they've endured. The steps already shared will need to take place before true forgiveness can come.

Don't let anyone rush you into this last part of the trip. The strength, confidence, self-worth, and self-acceptance are all attributes that God will use in your heart when the time of forgiveness comes. Remember, for everything there is a season.

As you move from one area of truth and recognition to another, we want to comfort you as our Lord comforted us (2 Corinthians 1:3-4). We share so that you might not feel alone along the way. You are not strange or bizarre because of what you have felt or seen; your pain is tender to our Lord for He has also traveled a path of sorrow. He was as familiar as you with the abuse of fellow human beings.

Sometimes the avenue to wholeness feels like major surgery. There are moments of pain so great that one may actually feel the cry of our Lord on Calvary, as he shouted, "My God, my God, why hast thou forsaken me?" At other junctures of the healing process you may experience such anger toward those who have hurt you that you cannot imagine ever being free from it or able to forgive.

Take courage, for other survivors before you and those yet to come have walked this same road. Our God looks upon the heart. Our emotions may scream, "I will never stop being angry or shamed," while our spirits cry out, "Lord, heal my wounded heart. Cleanse me and set me free from what was done to me. I want to be whole."

Jesus *felt* forsaken on the cross, yet He knew that His spirit trusted in and was entrusted to God the Father. He spoke honestly of what He felt. The healing journey will require that you do the same. As you do, remember that He, like the wounded child in us, was innocent and pure when the evil of humanity shamed Him and struck Him down. He knows your anger, sorrow, and grief even in those times when you can't seem to speak to Him. Even then, He will neither leave you nor forsake you, just as the Father did not leave Him. Are you afraid He won't understand the ugliness of what you have endured? Then perhaps you need to look across the road you are traveling for you will find Him there.

He, too, was a victim and a survivor. As you see Him here and there along the way, take courage and remember ". . . Him who endured such hostility by sinners against Himself, so that you [and I] may not grow weary and lose heart" (Hebrews 12:3).

May our Lord grant you the assurance of His love and mercy as you travel toward the valley of reality and the light of truth.

Denial/Shock

And I will lead the blind by a way they do not know, In paths they do not know I will guide them. I will make darkness into light before them And rugged places into plains. These are the things I will do, And I will not leave them undone.   *Isaiah 42:16*

I will go before you and make the rough places smooth; I will shatter the doors of bronze, and cut through their iron bars. And I will give you the treasures of darkness, And hidden wealth of secret places, In order that you may know that it is I, The Lord, the God of Israel, who calls you by your name.   *Isaiah 45:2-3*

". . . and you shall know the truth, and the truth shall make you free."
John 8:32

"Am I a God near by," says the Lord, "and not a God far off? Who can hide in secret places so that I cannot see them?" says the Lord. "Do I not fill the heaven and the earth?" says the Lord.
Jeremiah 23:23-24 (NRSV)

Behold, Thou dost desire truth in the innermost being, And in the hidden part Thou wilt make know wisdom.   *Psalm 51:6*

And I will make justice the measuring line, And righteousness the level; Then hail shall sweep away the refuge of lies, and the waters shall overflow the secret place. And your covenant with death shall be canceled, And your pact with Sheol shall not stand . . . .   *Isaiah 28:17-18b*

Where can I go from Thy Spirit? Or where can I flee from Thy presence? If I ascend to heaven, Thou art there; If I make my bed in Sheol, behold, Thou art there. If I take the wings of the dawn, If I dwell in the remotest part of the sea, Even there thy hand will lead me, And Thy right hand will lay hold of me. If I say, "Surely the darkness will overwhelm me, And the light around me will be night," even the darkness is not dark to thee, And the night is as bright as the day. Darkness and light are alike to Thee.   *Psalm 139:7-12*

Now Simon Peter was standing and warming himself. They said therefore to him, "You are not also one of His disciples, are you?" He denied it, and said, "I am not."   *John 18:25*

Do not lie to one another, since you laid aside the old self with its evil practices, and have put on the new self who is being renewed to a true knowledge according to the image of the One who created him, ...
    Colossians 3:9-10

Then I, Daniel, was exhausted and sick for days. Then I got up again and carried on the king's business; but I was astounded at the vision, and there was none to explain it.   *Daniel 8:27*

Look among the nations! Observe! Be astonished! Wonder! Because I am doing something in your days — You would not believe if you were told.   *Habakkuk 1:5*

It is not enemies who taunt me — I could bear that; it is not adversaries who deal insolently with me — I could hide from them. But it is you, my equal, my companion, my familiar friend, ...
    Psalm 55:12-13 (NRSV)

Happy are those who make the Lord their trust, who do not turn to the proud, to those who go astray after false gods.   *Psalm 40:4* (NRSV)

Keep deception and lies far from me, ...   *Proverbs 30:8a*

"But there is nothing covered up that will not be revealed, and hidden that will not be known."   *Luke 12:2*

Therefore do not pronounce judgment before the time, before the Lord comes, who will bring to light the things now hidden in darkness and will disclose the purposes of the heart. Then each one will receive commendation from God.   *1 Corinthians 4:5* (NRSV)

"Let them not trust in emptiness, deceiving themselves; for emptiness will be their recompense."   *Job 15:31* (NRSV)

But all things become visible when they are exposed by the light, for everything that becomes visible is light. For this reason it says, "Awake, sleeper, And arise from the dead, And Christ will shine on you."
Ephesians 5:13-14

Anger

BE ANGRY, AND *yet* DO NOT SIN; do not let the sun go down on your anger, and do not give the devil an opportunity.   *Ephesians 4:26-27*

Behold, I cry, Violence! but I get no answer; I shout for help, but there is no justice. He has walled up my way so that I cannot pass; And He has put darkness on my paths.   *Job 19:7-8*

. . . Moses' anger burned, and he threw the tablets from his hands and shattered them at the foot of the mountain.   *Exodus 32:20*

Hear, O our God, how we are despised! Return their reproach on their own heads and give them up for plunder in a land of captivity. Do not forgive their iniquity and let not their sin be blotted out before Thee, for they have demoralized the builders.   *Nehemiah 4:4-5*

Reproach has broken my heart, and I am so sick. And I looked for sympathy, but there was none, And for comforters, but I found none. Pour out Thine indignation on them, And may Thy burning anger overtake Them.   *Psalm 69:20, 24*

Contend, O Lord, with those who contend with me; Fight against those who fight against me. Take hold of buckler and shield, And rise up for my help.   *Psalm 35:1*

The wicked plot against the righteous, and gnash their teeth at them; but the Lord laughs at the wicked, for he sees that their day is coming. The wicked have drawn the sword and bent their bows to bring down poor and the needy, to kill those who walk uprightly; their sword will enter their own heart, And their bows shall be broken.

Psalm 37:12-15 (NRSV)

Evening and morning and at noon, I will complain and murmur, And He will hear my voice. He will redeem my soul in peace from the battle which is against me, For they are many who strive with me.

Psalm 55:17-18

They attack, they lurk, They watch my steps, As they have waited to take my life. Because of wickedness, cast them forth, In anger put down the peoples, O God!   *Psalm 56:6-7*

Oh God, shatter their teeth in their mouth; Break out the fangs of the young lions, O Lord. Let them flow away like water that runs off . . . let them be as a snail which melts away as it goes along . . . .

Psalm 56:67-7a, 8a

Your hand will find out all your enemies; your right hand will find out those who hate you. You will make them as a fiery furnace when you appear; The Lord will swallow them up in His wrath, and fire will consume them. You will destroy their offspring from the earth, and their children from among humankind. If they plan evil against you, if they devise mischief, they will not succeed. For you will put them to flight; you will aim at their faces with your bows. Be Thou exalted, O Lord, in your strength; We will sing and praise your power.   *Psalm 21:8-13*

Release

My voice rises to God, and I will cry aloud; My voice rises to God, and He will hear me. In the day of my trouble I sought the Lord; In the night my hand was stretched out without weariness; My soul refused to be comforted. When I remember God, then I am disturbed; When I sigh, then my spirit grows faint. Thou hast held my eyelids open; I am so troubled that I cannot speak . . . Then I said, It is my grief, That the right hand of the Most High has changed.   *Psalm 77:1-4, 10*

My soul weeps because of grief; Strengthen me according to Thy word.
     Psalm 119:28

It is not enemies who taunt me — I could bear that; it not adversaries who deal insolently with me — I could hide from them. But it is you, my equal, my companion, my familiar friend.   *Psalm 55:12-13* (NRSV)

. . . Weeping may last for the night, but a shout of joy comes in the morning.   *Psalm 30:5c*

But I am afflicted and needy; Hasten to me, O God! Thou art my help and my deliverer; O Lord, do not delay.   *Psalm 70:5*

Yet if any of you suffers as a Christian, do not consider it a disgrace, but glorify God because you bear this name. For the time has come for judgment to begin with the household of God; if it begins with us, what will be the end for those who do not obey the gospel of God? And "If it is hard for the righteous to be saved, what will become of the ungodly and the sinners?" Therefore, let those suffering in accordance with God's will entrust themselves to a faithful Creator, while continuing to do good.   *1 Peter 4:16-19* (NRSV)

For the Scripture says, "WHOEVER BELIEVES IN HIM WILL NOT BE DISAPPOINTED."   *Romans 10:11*

. . . those who hopefully wait for Me will not be put to shame.
Isaiah 49:23e

And immediately Jesus stretched out His hand and took hold of him, and said to him, "O you of little faith, why did you doubt?"
Matthew 14:31

And Jesus answered and said to them, "Truly I say to you, if you have faith, and do not doubt, ..."   *Matthew 21:21*

And when they saw Him, they worshiped Him; but some were doubtful.
Matthew 28:17

. . . who for the joy set before Him endured the cross, despising the shame . . . .   *Hebrews 12:2b*

Then they sat down on the ground with him for seven days and seven nights with no one speaking a word to him, for they saw that his pain was very great.   *Job 2:13*

O Lord, do not rebuke me in Thine anger, Nor chasten me in Thy wrath. Be gracious to me, O Lord, for I am pining away; Heal me, O Lord, for my bones are dismayed. And my soul is greatly dismayed; But Thou, O Lord — how long? Return, O Lord, rescue my soul; Save me because of Thy lovingkindness. For there is no mention of Thee in death; In Sheol who will give Thee thanks? I am weary with my sighing; Every night I make my bed swim, I dissolve my couch with my tears. My eye has wasted away with grief; It has become old because of all my adversaries. Depart from me, all you who do iniquity, For the Lord has heard the voice of my weeping. The Lord receives my prayer. All my enemies shall be ashamed and greatly dismayed; They shall turn back, they shall suddenly be ashamed.   *Psalm 6:1-10*

For these things I weep; My eyes run down with water; Because far from me is a comforter, One who restores my soul; My children are desolate Because the enemy has prevailed.   *Lamentations 2:16*

For the Lord has called you, Like a wife forsaken and grieved in spirit, Even like a wife of one's youth when she is rejected . . . .   *Isaiah 54:5*

Surely our griefs He Himself bore, And our sorrows He carried; Yet we ourselves esteemed Him stricken, Smitten of God, and afflicted.
Isaiah 53:4

Thus you will know that I am in the midst of Israel, And that I am the Lord your God And there is no other; And My people will never be put to shame.   *Joel 2:27*

Then I will make up to you for the years That the swarming locust has eaten, The creeping locust, the stripping locust, and the gnawing locust, ...   *Joel 2:25*

He heals the brokenhearted, And binds up their wounds. He counts the number of the stars; He gives names to all of them. Great is our Lord, and abundant in strength; His understanding is infinite. The Lord supports the afflicted; He brings down the wicked to the ground.
Psalm 147:3-6

Acceptance

The Lord is near to the brokenhearted, and saves the crushed in spirit. Many are the afflictions of the righteous; but the Lord rescues them from them all.   *Psalm 34:18-19* (NRSV)

Though the fig tree should not blossom, And there be no fruit on the vines, Though the yield of the olive shall fail, And the fields produce no food, Though the flock should be cut off from the fold, and there be no cattle in the stalls, Yet I will exult in the Lord, I will rejoice in the God of my salvation. The Lord God is my strength, And He has made my feet like hinds' feet, And makes me walk on my high places.

Habakkuk 3:17-19

Though He slay me, I will hope in Him. Nevertheless I will argue my ways before Him.   *Job 13:15*

I love Thee, O Lord, my strength. The Lord is my rock and my fortress and my deliverer, My God my rock, in whom I take refuge; My shield and the horn of my salvation, my stronghold. I call upon the Lord, who is worthy to be praised, And I am saved from my enemies.

Psalm 18:1-3

He sent from on high, He took me; He drew me out of many waters. He delivered me from my strong enemy, And from those who hated me, for they were too mighty for me. They confronted me in the day of my calamity, but the Lord was my stay. He brought me forth also into a broad place; He rescued me because He delighted in me.

Psalm 18:16-19

I appeal to you therefore, brothers and sisters, by the mercies of God, to present your bodies as a living sacrifice, holy and acceptable to God, which is your spiritual worship. Do not be conformed to this world, but be transformed by the renewing of your minds, so that you may discern what is the will of God — what is good and acceptable and perfect.

Romans 12:1-2 (NRSV)

And we know that God causes all things to work together for good to those who love God, to those who are called according to His purpose.

Romans 8:28

"And those are the ones on whom seed was sown on the good soil; and they hear the word and accept it, and bear fruit, thirty, sixty, and a hundredfold."   *Mark 4:20*

For as the rain and the snow come down from heaven, And do not return there without watering the earth, And making it bear and sprout, And furnishing seed to the sower and bread to the eater; So shall my word be which goes forth from My mouth; It shall not return to Me empty, Without accomplishing what I desire, And without succeeding in the matter for which I sent it. For you will go out with joy, And be led forth with peace; The mountains and the hills will break forth into shouts of joy before you, And all the trees of the field will clap their hands. Instead of the thorn bush the cypress will come up; And instead of the nettle the myrtle will come up; And it will be a memorial to the Lord, For an everlasting sign which will not be cut off.   *Isaiah 55:10-13*

For my father and my mother have forsaken me, But the Lord will take me up.   *Psalm 27:10*

". . . Shall we indeed accept good from God and not accept adversity?" In all this Job did not sin with his lips.   *Job 2:10b*

Forgiveness

Do not say, "I will repay evil"; Wait for the Lord, and He will save you.
Proverbs 20:22

But whom you forgive anything, I forgive also; for indeed what I have forgiven, if I have forgiven anything, I did it for your sakes in the presence of Christ, in order that no advantage be taken of us by Satan, for we are not ignorant of his schemes.   *2 Corinthians 2:10-11*

. . . "Father forgive them; for they do not know what they are doing."
. . . .   *Luke 23:34*

"But I say to you, love your enemies, and pray for those who persecute you."   *Matthew 5:44*

"For if you forgive others their trespasses, your heavenly Father will also forgive you; but if you do not forgive others, neither will your Father forgive your trespasses."   *Matthew 6:14-15* (NRSV)

In Him *we have* redemption through His blood, the *forgiveness* of our trespasses, according to the riches of His grace, ...   *Ephesians 1:7*

"And whenever you stand praying, forgive, if you have anything against anyone; so that your Father also who is in heaven may forgive you your transgressions."   *Mark 11:25*

Then Peter came and said to him, "Lord, if another member of the church sins against me, how often should I forgive? As many as seven times?" Jesus said to him, "Not seven times, but I tell you seventy-seven times. For this reason the kingdom of heaven may be compared to a king who wishes to settle accounts with his slaves. When he began the reckoning, one who owed him ten thousand talents was brought to him; and, as he could not pay, his lord ordered him to be sold, together with his wife and children and all his possessions, and payment to be made. So the slave fell on his knees before him, saying, 'Have patience with me, and I will pay you everything.' And out of pity for him, the lord of that slave released him and forgave him the debt. But that same slave, as he went out, came upon one of his fellow slaves who owed him a hundred denarii; and seizing him by the throat, he said, 'Pay back what you owe.' Then his fellow slave fell down and pleaded with him, 'Have patience with me and I will pay you.' But he refused; then he went and threw him into prison until he would pay the debt. When his fellow slaves saw what had happened, they were greatly distressed, and they went and reported to their lord all that had taken place. Then his lord summoned him and said to him, 'You wicked slave! I forgave you all that debt because you pleaded with me. Should you not have had mercy on your fellow slave, as I had mercy on you?' And in anger his lord handed him over to be tortured until he would pay his entire debt. So my heavenly Father will also do to every one of you, if you do not forgive your brother or sister from your heart."   *Matthew 18:21-35* (NRSV)

For He delivered us from the domain of darkness, and transferred us to the kingdom of His beloved Son, in whom we have redemption, the forgiveness of sins.   *Colossians 1:13-14*

Never take your own revenge, beloved, but leave room for the wrath of God, for it is written, "VENGEANCE IS MINE, I WILL REPAY," SAYS THE LORD. "BUT IF YOUR ENEMY IS HUNGRY, FEED HIM, AND IF HE IS THIRSTY, GIVE HIM A DRINK; FOR IN SO DOING YOU WILL HEAP BURNING COALS UPON HIS HEAD." Do not be overcome by evil, but overcome evil with good.

Romans 12:19-21

According to their deeds, so He will repay, Wrath to His adversaries, recompense to His enemies; . . . .   *Isaiah 59:18*

There is an appointed time for everything. And there is a time for every event under heaven — A time to give birth, and a time to die; A time to plant, and a time to uproot what is planted. A time to kill, and a time to heal; A time to tear down, and a time to build up. A time to weep, and a time to laugh; A time to mourn, and a time to dance. A time to throw stones, and a time to gather stones; A time to embrace, and a time to shun embracing. A time to search, and a time to give up as lost; A time to keep, and a time to throw away. A time to tear apart, and a time to sew together; A time to be silent, and a time to speak. A time to love, and a time to hate; A time for war, and a time for peace.   *Ecclesiastes 3:1-8*

"And forgive us our debts, as we also have forgiven our debtors."

Matthew 6:12

And be kind to one another, tender-hearted, forgiving each other, just as God in Christ also has forgiven you.   *Ephesians 4:32*

To the Lord our God belong compassion and forgiveness, ...

Daniel 9:9

If Thou, Lord, shouldst mark iniquities, O Lord, who could stand? but there is forgiveness with Thee, ...   *Psalm 130:3-4a*

"Blessed are the merciful, for they shall receive mercy."   *Matthew 5:7*

HEALING **JOURNAL**
leg 16 / denial / shock

Use this page to record your personal thoughts and reflections.

leg 16 / denial / shock

Use this page to record your special Bible verses that encourage you on the journey (verses need not be limited to the ones in this book).

HEALING **JOURNAL**
leg 17 / anger

Use this page to record your personal thoughts and reflections.

HEALING **JOURNAL**
leg 17 / anger

Use this page to record your personal thoughts and reflections.

HEALING **JOURNAL**
leg 18 / release

Use this page to record your personal thoughts and reflections.

leg 18 / release

Use this page to record your special Bible verses that encourage you on the journey (verses need not be limited to the ones in this book).

HEALING **JOURNAL**
leg 19 / acceptance

Use this page to record your personal thoughts and reflections.

leg 19 / acceptance

Use this page to record your special Bible verses that encourage you on the journey (verses need not be limited to the ones in this book).

HEALING **JOURNAL**
leg 20 / forgiveness

Use this page to record your personal thoughts and reflections.

leg 20 / forgiveness

Use this page to record your special Bible verses that encourage you on the journey (verses need not be limited to the ones in this book).

4
OBSTACLES

Wouldn't it be nice if there were journeys free of obstacles? Unfortunately, that is seldom the case. There are times when your bags don't arrive at the same time you do. Sometimes hotel reservations are lost. Many complain that rental cars are not there when needed, and isn't it upsetting when you run out of money or lose your credit cards? On occasion the beds are too hard, the pillows too soft, and the food is unpalatable.

The following definitions will help you pinpoint areas that may surface to frustrate your healing journey. If you recognize possible problems before starting out, you are more able to face and overcome each one.

Discouragement. A sense of discouragement comes when you feel it isn't worth fighting the battle anymore. You are tired and disillusioned and wonder if the pain is worth the outcome.

False pride. This feeling often comes when you don't want anyone else to help you. "I can do this all by myself" is usually the response. For some, the attitude is "What can anyone else possibly do for me that I can't do for myself?" Others argue that such things couldn't possibly have happened in families such as theirs. These mistaken presumptions can cause you to cease to deal with the truth and become bogged down in denial.

Compromise.   Compromise is a great enemy of recovery. This subtle opponent tries to convince you that help isn't really necessary. You cannot compromise what is right just to stop the pain involved in the battle for wholeness. Such a stance might express itself in words like this: "Why should I bother to go through this unpleasantness of learning to feel when I can just go eat, drink, or buy something? These things make me happy. Why put myself in a place of potential suffering when I know I can get comfort in other ways?"

Aimlessness.   During times when you have no goals or objectives, a sensation of aimlessness often seems overwhelming. You may ask, "What is going to come from all of this? I don't know where it's leading me. It seems like I'm just wandering through a maze and there doesn't appear to be an end or a reward."

Ridicule.   How often have you come face to face with this adversary? Others don't understand. Some actually may tell you that you must be unstable if you consider the road to healing. What pain can be inflicted by such a thoughtless response! It is no easy thing to stand in the face of ridicule especially when it comes from those who profess to care for you.

Rejection.   Like ridicule, this attacker can overpower even the strongest survivor. Rejection can come in so many different forms and from so many different people. Some families reject the survivor for even looking into the past. Friends may not like the healthy changes that begin to take place since some of these relationships are based on unhealthy needs and responses. Not everyone wants to be whole and those who don't have such a desire may be threatened by your stand to grow. Others may reject you because the issues you face might force them to confront unpleasantness buried within themselves.

Unbelief.   When you are working through your abuse, it is safe to say that you will encounter times of unbelief. Such questions as, "How can God have allowed this to happen to me?" or "What kind of God could say He loved me and let me experience such agony?" are frequently asked by survivors. They are normal. While these are difficult questions, you must pass through them and come to peace with your own answers before moving on to the next step of the healing journey. You are no less a Christian because you allow those buried angry questions finally to express themselves. They are a part of being human. If that is a crime then you are guilty — guilty of the humanity that God gave you. Don't let the desert of unbelief that accompanies the healing of deep wounds make you accept the lie that you don't belong to Jesus. He will give you a new depth of awareness concerning who He is after you have passed through the dry places. Your emotions may say, "I don't want to believe in God anymore," but your spirit still cries out, "Lord please don't let go of me."

Impatience.   What a stumbling block to recovery! So many travelers want to reach the destination immediately. Some may contact a counselor only to demand that everything be "fixed" in a few short sessions. If the process doesn't flow according to plan, some want to quit. Unfortunately your abuse takes time, trust, fellowship, counsel, and the touch of our Lord to repair. Demanding quick results only prolongs the course and makes the goal seem more and more distant. Try to work through these bouts of impatience or they may cause detours along the way.

Hopelessness.   Every victim or survivor struggles against hopelessness. Such despair surfaces when the memories don't come as you had hoped or when the feelings of pain appear to continue too long. Often hopelessness is a response when you don't feel like you are progressing at all. Hopelessness tells you that there is no end to the journey and that you will forever be as you are today. This is yet another lie from the enemy of your soul. Don't let the deceiver turn a trail to victory into a path of despair by luring you into a false sense of hopelessness.

Mistrust.   One of the hardest emotions for a victim to grasp is trust. When you have been abused by trusted family members or friends during childhood, there doesn't appear to be anyone left worth trusting. Sadly, such a survivor finds it almost impossible to trust him or herself. To trust again after such woundedness is a monumental step.

Sometimes it takes months to trust a counselor, pastor, or therapist. These are fragile times as you begin to reach inside and let that little one of your heart try to trust again. Don't be too hard on yourself if it takes time. Many others have learned to be vulnerable and trusting after victimization. You are not alone and there is nothing peculiar about having to learn to trust. Remember while you travel down the road to freedom that pain, anger, grief, and sorrow are being released to enable you to trust once more.

Temporary relief.   Exciting events like a new marriage, baby, home, car, or friend can provide moments of temporary relief. The addictions discussed earlier can also bring momentary comfort. None of these is the answer to your heartache. Some victims are willing to forfeit final freedom by stopping at the first sign of consolation. Unfortunately, temporary relief is just that. When it is over, the pathway still lies before you. These distractions have not and cannot heal your heart.

Self-pity.   Another enemy of your journey will be self-pity. This foe tries to woo you into believing that no one else has ever been hurt as you have. Taunting inner whispers such as, "How could anyone hurt you like that and then expect you to function in this world?" and "God must love other Christians more because they don't seem to have awful problems like mine" only stifle you and frustrate forward progress. It's like quicksand that pulls you under as fast as you try to climb out. Be on guard for this hypocrite whose design is to focus your eyes on futility rather than freedom.

Unworthiness.   How many times have you felt unworthy to be loved, to be respected, *to be free*? Survivors all pass through this dark tunnel. When abuse has been endured, it leaves the victim with a sense of inadequacy. Most feel they don't deserve anything good in life. As the healing journey progresses, there will be times when you feel unworthy of the work God is doing in your heart. These, too, are appropriate responses after all you have been through. As restoring light begins to stream into your soul, you will at last see His face. Only then can you find your true worth for it is fully reflected there.

Until that time, you will need to battle any thoughts of unworthiness that try to discourage your pilgrimage. As you learn to pour out the pain of yesterday's child, you will discover a true and healthy personal worth. Don't allow anything to deter you from your goal of recovery.

Fear.   Perhaps one of the most powerful obstacles in your journey is fear. There are so many potential doorways for this antagonist to walk through. Victims can become bogged down by the fears of remembering, pain, trusting, exposure and embarrassment, and so on.

No healing journey is free of fear. Your past abuse has created an arena of fright and alarm within.

Some victims develop a sense of what is called *hypervigilance.* This state causes you to avert any hint of danger, while constantly expecting it. These thoughts are all rooted in your abuse. Imagine how difficult it could be to reach your destination when such fear consumes you.

While fear is a natural response to what happened to you in the past, there are tools to release those fear-packed memories now. You no longer need to expect the worst. Once the journey of wholeness becomes real to you, unhealthy fears will gradually disappear. Even an obstacle as powerful as fear can ultimately be turned into assurance and security.

Vengefulness.   While it is absolutely imperative that you recognize these vengeful feelings welling up inside, you must also allow them to pass when the time is right. Vengefulness is like an ulcer: It hurts no one more than its container. Too often you hold onto revenge and are blinded by the truth that this aspect of retribution belongs to God. It is as if He waits for us to give those vindictive cravings to Him before He really begins to administer justice. He is far more able to extract what is owed than you or I. Can you trust Him to relieve you of that destructive burden?

The following verses have been compiled by others who have known abuse. The obstacles described previously were battled by each one. May the words God tenderly spoke to past survivors bring comfort and relief to your heart. As each verse becomes real to you, write the date in the margin. This log of your journey will be a lasting testimony to the power of God in your life.

Discouragement

For all of them were *trying* to frighten us, thinking, "They will become discouraged with the work and it will not be done." But now, *O God, strengthen my hands.*   *Nehemiah 6:9*

For I want you to know how great a struggle I have on your behalf, and for those who are at Laodicea, and for all those who have not personally seen my face, that their hearts may be encouraged, having been knit together in love, and *attaining* to all the wealth that comes from the full assurance of understanding, *resulting* in a true knowledge of God's mystery, *that is,* Christ *Himself*, ...   *Colossians 2:1-2*

And he is before all things, and in Him all things hold together.
                                                                                  Colossians 1:17

"The afflicted and needy are seeking water, but there is none, And their tongue is parched with thirst; I, the Lord, will answer them Myself, *As the God of Israel I will not forsake them. I will open rivers on the bare heights, And springs in the midst of the valleys; I will make the wilderness a pool of water, And the dry land fountains of water."

Isaiah 41:17-18

"O afflicted one, storm-tossed, and not comforted, . . . All your children shall be taught by the Lord, and great shall be the prosperity of your children. In righteousness you shall be established; you shall be far from oppression, for you shall not fear; and from terror, for it shall not come near you. If anyone stirs up strife, it is not from me; whoever stirs up strife with you shall fall because of you. See it is I who have created the smith who blows the fire of coals, and produces a weapon fit for its purpose; I have also created the ravager to destroy. No weapon that is fashioned against you shall prosper, and you shall confute every tongue that rises against you in judgment. This is the heritage of the servants of the Lord, And their vindication is from me," declares the Lord.

Isaiah 54:11-17 (NRSV)

O Lord, how my adversaries have increased! Many are rising up against me. Many are saying of my soul, "There is no deliverance for him in God." But Thou, O Lord, art a shield about me, My glory, and the One who lifts my head. I was crying to the Lord with my voice, And He answered me from His holy mountain. I lay down and slept; I awoke, for the Lord sustains me. I will not be afraid of ten thousands of people Who have set themselves against me round about. Arise, O Lord; save me, O my God! For Thou hast smitten all my enemies on the cheek; Thou hast shattered the teeth of the wicked. Salvation belongs to the Lord; Thy blessing *be* upon Thy people!   *Psalm 3:1-8*

Who executes justice for the oppressed; Who gives food to the hungry. The Lord sets the prisoners free. The Lord opens *the eyes of* the blind; The Lord raises up those who are bowed down; The Lord loves the righteous;   *Psalm 146:7-8*

Light arises in the darkness for the upright; *He is* gracious and compassionate and righteous.   *Psalm 112:4*

But in all these things we overwhelmingly conquer through Him who loved us.   *Romans 8:37*

From the end of the earth I call to Thee, when my heart is faint; Lead me to the rock that is higher than I.   *Psalm 61:2*

Why are you in despair, O my soul? And *why* have you become disturbed within me? Hope in God, for I shall again praise Him *For* the help of His presence.   *Psalm 42:5*

. . . I pray that, according to the riches of his glory, he may grant that you may be strengthened in your inner being with power through his Spirit, and that Christ may dwell in your hearts through faith, as you are being rooted and grounded in love, ...   *Ephesians 3:16-17* (NRSV)

I would have despaired unless I had believed that I would see the goodness of the Lord In the land of the living. Wait for the Lord; Be strong, and let your heart take courage; Yes, wait for the Lord.
                                                                    Psalm 27:13-14

But now, thus says the Lord, your Creator, O Jacob, And He who formed you, O Israel, "Do not fear, for I have redeemed you; I have called you by name; you are Mine! When you pass through the waters, I will be with you; And through the rivers, they will not overflow you. When you walk through the fire, you will not be scorched, Nor will the flame burn you. For I am the Lord your God, The Holy One of Israel, your Savior; . . . ."   *Isaiah 43:1-3a*

. . . Thus says the Lord, the God of your father David, "I have heard your prayer, I have seen your tears; behold, I will heal you." . . .   *2 Kings 20:5a*

. . . and if children, heirs also, heirs of God and fellow heirs with Christ, if indeed we suffer with *Him.* For I consider that the sufferings of this present time are not worthy to be compared with the glory that is to be revealed to us.   *Romans 8:17-18*

Pride

"For My thoughts are not your thoughts, Neither are your ways My ways," declares the Lord. "For *as* the heavens are higher than the earth, So are My ways higher than your ways, And My thoughts than your thoughts. For as the rain and the snow come down from heaven, And do not return there without watering the earth, And making it bear and sprout, And furnishing seed to the sower and bread to the eater;"

Isaiah 55:8-10

"O Jerusalem, Jerusalem, who kills the prophets and stones those who are sent to her! How often I wanted to gather your children together, the way a hen gathers her chicks under her wings, and you are unwilling."

Matthew 23:37

Or do you think that the Scripture speaks to no purpose: "He jealously desires the Spirit which He has made to dwell in us?" But He gives a greater grace. Therefore *it* says, "God is opposed to the proud, but gives grace to the humble." *James 4:5-6*

Behold, Thou dost desire truth in the innermost being, And in the hidden part Thou wilt make me know wisdom. *Psalm 51:6*

Through presumption comes nothing but strife, But with those who receive counsel is wisdom. *Proverbs 13:10*

When pride comes, then comes dishonor, But with the humble is wisdom. *Proverbs 11:2*

"Let them not trust in emptiness, deceiving themselves; for emptiness will be their recompense." *Job 15:31*

Trust in the Lord with all your heart, And do not lean on your own understanding. *Proverbs 3:5*

Do not put your trust in princes, in mortals, in whom there is no help. When their breath departs, they return to the earth; on that very day their plans perish. Happy are those whose help is the God of Jacob, whose hope is in the Lord their God.   *Psalm 146:3-5 (NRSV)*

Unless the Lord builds the house, those who build it labor in vain. Unless the Lord guards the city, the guard keeps watch in vain. It is in vain that you rise up early and go late to rest, eating the bread of anxious toil; for he gives to his beloved *even in his* sleep.   *Psalm 127:1-2*

All one's ways may be pure in one's own eyes, but the Lord weighs the spirit.   *Proverbs 16:2*

All deeds are right in the sight of the doer, but the Lord weighs the heart.   *Proverbs 21:2 (NRSV)*

A person's pride will bring humiliation, but one who is lowly in spirit will obtain honor.   *Proverbs 29:23 (NRSV)*

O love the Lord, all you His godly ones! The Lord preserves the faithful, And fully recompenses the proud doer.   *Psalm 31:23*

Woe to those who are wise in their own eyes, And clever in their own sight!   *Isaiah 5:21*

Thou hast also given me the shield of Thy salvation, And Thy right hand upholds me; And Thy gentleness makes me great.   *Psalm 18:35*

Compromise

The refining pot is for silver and the furnace for gold, But the Lord tests hearts.   *Proverbs 17:3*

Happy are those who do not follow the advice of the wicked, or take the path that sinners tread, or sit in the seat of scoffers; but their delight is in the law of the Lord, and on his law they meditate day and night. They are like trees planted by streams of water, which yield their fruit in its season, and their leaves do not wither. In all that they do, they prosper.

Psalm 1:1-3 (NRSV)

"But seek first His kingdom and His righteousness; and all these things shall be added to you."   *Matthew 6:33*

Anyone, then, who knows the right thing to do and fails to do it, commits sin.   *James 4:17* (NRSV)

I urge you, brothers and sisters, to keep an eye on those who cause dissensions and offenses, in opposition to the teaching that you have learned; avoid them. For such people do not serve our Lord Christ, but their own appetites, and by smooth talk and flattery they deceive the hearts of the simple-minded.   *Romans 16:17-18* (NRSV)

They speak falsehood to one another; With flattering lips and with a double heart they speak.   *Psalm 12:2*

If any of you is lacking in wisdom, ask God, who gives to all generously and ungrudgingly, and it will be given you. But ask in faith, never doubting, for the one who doubts is like a wave of the sea, driven and tossed by the wind; for the doubter, being double-minded and unstable in every way, must not expect to receive anything from the Lord.

James 1:5-8 (NRSV)

"But let your statement be, 'Yes, yes' *or* 'No, no'; and anything beyond these is of evil."   *Matthew 5:37*

Above all, my beloved, do not swear, either by heaven or by earth or by any other oath, but let your "Yes" be yes, and your "No" be no, so that you may not fall under condemnation.   *James 5:12* (NRSV)

"For what will it profit them if they gain the whole world but forfeit their life? Or what will they give in return for their life?"
Matthew 16:26 (NRSV)

For even though they knew God, they did not honor Him as God, or give thanks; but they became futile in their speculations, and their foolish heart was darkened. Professing to be wise, they became fools, ...
Romans 1:21-22

There is a way that seems right to a person, but its end is the way to death.   *Proverbs 14:12* (NRSV)

Those who are greedy for unjust gain make trouble for their households, but those who hate bribes will live.   *Proverbs 15:27* (NRSV)

All one's ways may be pure in one's own eyes, but the Lord weighs the spirit.   *Proverbs 16:2* (NRSV)

By faith Moses, when he had grown up, refused to be called the son of Pharaoh's daughter; choosing rather to endure ill-treatment with the people of God, than to enjoy the passing pleasures of sin; . . . .
Hebrews 11:24-25

"And the one on whom seed was sown among the thorns, this is the man who hears the word, and the worry of the world, and the deceitfulness of riches choke the word, and it becomes unfruitful."   *Matthew 13:22*

Aimlessness

Do you not know that those who run in a race all run, but *only* one receives the prize? Run in such a way that you may win. And everyone who competes in the games exercises self-control in all things. They then *do it* to receive a perishable wreath, but we an imperishable. Therefore I run in such a way, as not without aim; I box in such a way, As not beating the air; but I buffet my body and make it my slave, lest possibly, after I have preached to others, I myself should be disqualified.

1 Corinthians 9:24-27

For Thou dost light my lamp; The Lord my God illumines my darkness.

Psalm 18:28

Thus says the Lord, your Redeemer, the Holy One of Israel; "I am the Lord your God, who teaches you to profit, Who leads you in the way you should go."   *Isaiah 48:17*

I will instruct you and teach you in the way which you should go; I will counsel you with My eye upon you.   *Psalm 32:8*

O send out thy light and Thy truth, let them lead me; Let them bring me to Thy holy hill, And to Thy dwelling places.   *Psalm 43:3*

"Does He not see my ways, And number all my steps?   *Job 31:4*

Therefore the Lord longs to be gracious to you, And therefore He waits on high to have compassion on you. For the Lord is a God of justice; How blessed are all those who long for Him.   *Isaiah 30:18*

"For the Lord your God has blessed you in all that you have done; He has known your wanderings through this great wilderness. These forty years the Lord your God has been with you; you have not lacked a thing."   *Deuteronomy 2:7*

Thy testimonies are righteous forever; Give me understanding that I may live.   *Psalm 119:144*

But ask in faith, never doubting, for the one who doubts is like a wave of the sea, driven and tossed by the wind; for the doubter, being double-minded and unstable in every way, must not expect to receive anything from the Lord.   *James 1:6-8* (NRSV)

For God has not called us for the purpose of impurity, but in sanctification.   *1 Thessalonians 4:7*

"I know that Thou canst do all things, And that no purpose of Thine can be thwarted."   *Job 42:2*

Declaring the end from the beginning And from ancient times things which have not been done, Saying, "My purpose will be established, And I will accomplish all My good pleasure"; Calling a bird of prey from the east, The man of My purpose from a far country. Truly I have spoken; truly I will bring it to pass. I have planned *it, surely* I will do it.
Isaiah 46:10-11

And we know that God causes all things to work together for good to those who love God, to those who are called according to *His* purpose.
Romans 8:28

Therefore, I was not vacillating when I intended to do this, was I? Or that which I purpose, do I purpose according to the flesh, that with me there should be yes, yes and no, no at the same time?
2 Corinthians 1:17

Now He who prepares us for this very purpose is God, who gave to us the Spirit as a pledge.   *2 Corinthians 5:5*

. . . also we have obtained an inheritance, having been predestined according to His purpose who works all things after the counsel of His will, ...   *Ephesians 1:11*

... make my joy complete by being of the same mind, maintaining the same love, united in spirit, intent on one purpose.   *Philippians 2:2*

For you have been called for this purpose, since Christ also suffered for you, leaving you an example for you to follow in His steps, ...
1 Peter 2:21

... not returning evil for evil, or insult for insult, but giving a blessing instead; for you were called for the very purpose that you might inherit a blessing.   *1 Peter 3:9*

Therefore, since Christ has suffered in the flesh, arm yourselves also with the same purpose, because he who has suffered in the flesh has ceased from sin, ...   *1 Peter 4:1*

Ridicule

"For I will restore you to health And I will heal you of your wounds," declares the Lord, "Because they have called you an outcast, saying: . . . no one cares for her."   *Jeremiah 30:17*

I will extol Thee, O Lord, for Thou hast lifted me up, And hast not let my enemies rejoice over me. O Lord my God, I cried to Thee for help, and Thou didst heal me. O Lord, Thou hast brought up my soul from Sheol; Thou hast kept me alive, that I should not go down to the pit.
Psalm 30:3

But God has chosen the foolish things of the world to shame the wise, and God has chosen the weak things of the world to shame the things which are strong.   *1 Corinthians 1:27*

Be gracious to us, O Lord, be gracious to us; For we are greatly filled with contempt. Our soul is greatly filled With the scoffing of those who are at ease, *And* with the contempt of the proud.   *Psalm 123:3-4*

But as for me, I will watch expectantly for the Lord; I will wait for the God of my salvation. My God will hear me. Do not rejoice over me, O my enemy. Though I fall I will rise; Though I dwell in darkness, the Lord is a light for me.   *Micah 7:7-8*

For I am convinced that neither death, nor life, nor angels, nor principalities, not things present, nor things to come, nor powers, nor height, nor depth, nor any other created thing, shall be able to separate us from the love of God, which is in Christ Jesus our Lord.   *Romans 8:38-39*

And the God of peace will soon crush Satan under your feet. The grace of our Lord Jesus be with you.   *Romans 16:20*

For he did not despise or abhor the affliction of the afflicted; he did not hide his face from me, but heard when I cried to him.
    Psalm 22:24 (NRSV)

He has regarded the prayer of the destitute, And has not despised their prayer.   *Psalm 102:17*

. . . and the base things of the world and the despised, God has chosen, the things that are not, that He might nullify the things that are, ...
    2 Corinthians 1:28

Hear, O our God, how we are despised! Return their reproach on their own heads and give them up for plunder in a land of captivity. Do not forgive their iniquity and let not their sin be blotted out before Thee, for they have demoralized the builders.   *Nehemiah 4:4-5*

"My friends are my scoffers; My eye weeps to God."   *Job 16:20*

Though He scoffs at the scoffers, Yet He gives grace to the afflicted.

Proverbs 3:34

"Behold, you scoffers, and marvel, and perish; For I am accomplishing a work in your days, A work which you will never believe, though someone should describe it to you."   *Acts 13:41*

Our soul is greatly filled With the scoffing of those who are at ease, *And* with the contempt of the proud.   *Psalm 123:4*

Rejection

Let your character be free from the love of money, being content with what you have; for He Himself has said, "I will never desert you, nor will I ever forsake you."   *Hebrews 13:5*

For he did not despise or abhor the affliction of the afflicted; he did not hide his face from me, but heard when I cried to him.

Psalm 22:24 (NRSV)

And those who know Thy name will put their trust in Thee; For Thou, O Lord, has not forsaken those who seek Thee.   *Psalm 9:10*

But Zion said, "The Lord has forsaken me, And the Lord has forgotten me. Can a woman forget her nursing child, And have no compassion on the son of her womb? Even these may forget, but I will not forget you. Behold, I have inscribed you on the palms *of My hands*; Your walls are continually before Me."   *Isaiah 49:14-16*

"If your outcasts are at the ends of the earth, from there the Lord your God will gather you, and from there He will bring you back."

Deuteronomy 30:4

"And now do not be grieved or angry with yourselves, because you sold me here; for God sent me before you to preserve life."   *Genesis 45:5*

"You are My servant, I have chosen you and not rejected you. Do not fear, for I am with you; Do not anxiously look about you, for I am your God. I will strengthen you, surely I will help you, Surely I will uphold you with My righteous right hand. Behold, all those who are angered at you will be shamed and dishonored; Those who contend with you will be as nothing, and will perish. You will seek those who quarrel with you, but will not find them, Those who war with you will be as nothing, and non-existent. For I am the Lord your God, who upholds your right hand, Who says to you, 'Do not fear, I will help you.' "   *Isaiah 41:8-13*

Hear, O Lord, when I cry with my voice, And be gracious to me and answer me. *When Thou didst say,* "Seek My face," my heart said to Thee, "Thy face, O Lord, I shall seek. Do not hide Thy face from me, Do not turn Thy servant away in anger; Thou hast been my help; Do not abandon me nor forsake me, O God of my salvation! For my father and my mother have forsaken me, But the Lord will take me up."
Psalm 27:8-10

"Moreover, I will make My dwelling among you, and My soul will not reject you."   *Leviticus 26:11*

"Lo, God will not reject *a man of* integrity, Nor will He support the evildoers."   *Job 8:20*

Do not cast me away from Thy presence, And do not take Thy Holy Spirit from me.   *Psalm 51:11*

"Blessed are those who have been persecuted for righteousness' sake, for theirs is the kingdom of heaven. Blessed are you when people revile you and persecute you and utter all kinds of evil against you falsely, on my account. Rejoice, and be glad, for your reward is great in heaven, for in the same way they persecuted the prophets who were before you."
Matthew 5:10-12 (NRSV)

"Be strong and courageous, do not be afraid or tremble at them, for the Lord your God is the one who goes with you. He will not fail you or forsake you."   *Deuteronomy 31:6*

"And the Lord is the one who goes ahead of you; He will be with you. He will not fail you or forsake you. Do not fear, or be dismayed."

Deuteronomy 31:8

Thou, in Thy great compassion, Didst not forsake them in the wilderness; The pillar of cloud did not leave them by day, To guide them on their way, Nor the pillar of fire by night, to light for them the way in which they were to go.   *Nehemiah 9:19*

Do not hide Thy face from me, Do not turn Thy servant away in anger; Thou hast been my help; Do not abandon me nor forsake me, O God of my salvation!   *Psalm 27:9*

For the Lord loves justice, And does not forsake His godly ones; They are preserved forever; But the descendants of the wicked will be cut off.

Psalm 37:28

"The afflicted and needy are seeking water, but there is none, And their tongue is parched with thirst; I, the Lord, will answer them Myself, *As* the God of Israel I will not forsake them."   *Isaiah 41:17*

Better is open rebuke Than love that is concealed.   *Proverbs 27:5*

And coming to Him as to a living stone, rejected by men, but choice and precious in the sight of God, you also, as living stones, are being built up as a spiritual house . . . .   *1 Peter 2:4-5a*

Unbelief

Our steps are made firm by the Lord, when he delights in our way; though we stumble, we shall not fall headlong, for the Lord holds us by the hand.　*Psalm 37:23* (NRSV)

"Call to Me, and I will answer you, and I will tell you great and mighty things, which you do not know."　*Jeremiah 33;3*

. . . yet, with respect to the promise of God, he did not waver in unbelief, but grew strong in faith, giving glory to God, and being fully assured that what He had promised, He was able also to perform.　*Romans 4:20-21*

Therefore, do not throw away your confidence, which has a great reward. For you have need of endurance, so that when you have done the will of God, you may receive what was promised.　*Hebrews 10:35-36*

And He did not do many miracles there because of their unbelief.
　　　　　　　　　　　　　　　　　　　　　Matthew 13:58

Immediately the boy's father cried out and *began* saying, "I do believe; help my unbelief."　*Mark 9:24*

And afterward He appeared to the eleven themselves as they were reclining *at the table*; and He reproached them for their unbelief and hardness of heart, because they had not believed those who had seen Him after He had risen.　*Mark 16:14*

What then? If some did not believe, their unbelief will not nullify the faithfulness of God, will it?　*Romans 3:3*

In spite of all this they still sinned, And did not believe in His wonderful works.   *Psalm 78:32*

Jesus said to her, "Did I not say to you, if you believe, you will see the glory of God?"   John 11:40

And immediately Jesus stretched out His hand and took hold of him, and said to him, "O you of little faith, why did you doubt?"

Matthew 14:31

And Jesus answered and said to them, "Truly I say to you, if you have faith, and do not doubt, you shall not only do what was done to the fig tree, but even if you say to this mountain, 'Be taken up and cast into the sea,' it shall happen."   *Matthew 21:21*

"Truly I tell you, if you say to this mountain, 'Be taken up and thrown into the sea,' and if you do not doubt in your heart, but believe that what you say will come to pass, it will be done for you."

Mark 11:23 (NRSV)

But ask in faith, never doubting, for the one who doubts is like the wave of the sea, driven and tossed by the wind; . . . .   *James 1:6* (NRSV)

But you, beloved, building yourselves up on your most holy faith; praying in the Holy Spirit; keep yourselves in the love of God, waiting anxiously for the mercy of our Lord Jesus Christ to eternal life. And have mercy on some, who are doubting; . . . .   *Jude 1:20-22*

And He said to them, "Why are you troubled, and why do doubts arise in your hearts?"   *Luke 24:38*

"If I told you earthly things and you do not believe, how shall you believe if I tell you heavenly things?"   *John 3:12*

Impatience

I wait for the Lord, my soul does wait, And in His word do I hope. My soul *waits* for the Lord More than the watchmen for the morning; *Indeed, more than* the watchmen for the morning.   *Psalm 130:5-6*

Do not go out hastily to argue your case; Otherwise, what will you do in the end, When your neighbor puts you to shame?   *Proverbs 25:8*

How long shall I take counsel in my soul, *Having* sorrow in my heart all the day? How long will my enemy be exalted over me?   *Psalm 13:2*

I would have despaired unless I had believed that I would see the goodness of the Lord In the land of the living. Wait for the Lord; Be strong, and let your heart take courage; Yes, wait for the Lord.   *Psalm 27:13-14*

Therefore the Lord longs to be gracious to you, And therefore He waits on high to have compassion on you. For the Lord is a God of justice; How blessed are all those who long for Him.   *Isaiah 30:18*

I waited patiently for the Lord; And He inclined to me, and heard my cry. He brought me up out of the pit of destruction, out of the miry clay; And He set my feet upon a rock making my footsteps firm. And He put a new song in my mouth, a song of praise to our God; Many will see and fear, And will trust in the Lord.   *Psalm 40:1-3*

Be still before the Lord, and wait patiently for him; do not fret over those who prosper in their way, over those who carry out evil devices.
     Psalm 37:7 (NRSV)

Be patient, therefore, beloved, until the coming of the Lord. The farmer waits for the precious produce crop from the earth, being patient with it until it receives the early and the late rains. You also must be patient. Strengthen your hearts, for the coming of the Lord is near.   *James 5:7-8* (NRSV)

"By your endurance you will gain your lives."   *Luke 21:19*

Therefore, do not throw away your confidence, which has a great reward. For you have need of endurance, so that when you have done the will of God, you may receive what was promised.   *Hebrews 10:35-36*

. . . knowing that the testing of your faith produces endurance. And let endurance have *its* perfect result, that you may be perfect and complete, lacking in nothing.   *James 1:3-4*

"Cease *striving* and know that I am God; I will be exalted among the nations, I will be exalted in the earth."   *Psalm 46:10*

Yet those who wait for the Lord Will gain new strength; They will mount up *with* wings like eagles, They will run and not get tired, They will walk and not become weary.   *Isaiah 40:31*

But the fruit of the Spirit is love, joy, peace, patience, kindness, goodness, faithfulness, ...   *Galatians 5:22*

And so, as those who have been chosen of God, holy and beloved, put on a heart of compassion, kindness, humility, gentleness and patience; . . . .
                                                            Colossians 3:12

. . . that you may not be sluggish, but imitators of those who through faith and patience inherit the promises.   *Hebrews 6:12*

As an example, brethren, of suffering and patience, take the prophets who spoke in the name of the Lord.   *James 5:10*

Indeed, none of those who wait for Thee will be ashamed; Those who deal treacherously without cause will be ashamed. Lead me in Thy truth and teach me, For Thou art the God of my salvation; For Thee I wait all the day.   *Psalm 25:4-5*

Wait for the Lord, and keep His way, And He will exalt you to inherit the land; When the wicked are cut off, you will see it.   *Psalm 37:34*

"And now, Lord, for what do I wait? My hope is in Thee."

Psalm 39:7

My soul, wait in silence for God only, For my hope is from Him.

Psalm 62:5

May those who wait for Thee not be ashamed through me, O Lord God of hosts; May those who seek Thee not be dishonored through me, O God of Israel, ...   *Psalm 69:6*

The Lord favors those who fear Him, Those who wait for His loving-kindness.   *Psalm 147:11*

Do not say, "I will repay evil"; Wait for the Lord, and He will save you.

Proverbs 20:22

Those who hopefully wait for Me will not be put to shame.

Isaiah 49:23c

But as for me, I will watch expectantly for the Lord; I will wait for the God of my salvation. My God will hear me.   *Micah 7:7*

"For the vision is yet for the appointed time; It hastens toward the goal, and it will not fail. Though it tarries, wait for it; For it will certainly come, it will not delay."   *Habakkuk 2:3*

But if we hope for what we do not see, with perseverance we wait eagerly for it.   *Romans 8:25*

Therefore do not pronounce judgment before the time, before the Lord comes, who will bring to light the things now hidden in darkness and will disclose the purposes of the heart.   *1 Corinthians 4:5* (NRSV)

Hopelessness

The Lord is near to all who call upon Him, To all who call upon Him in truth. He will fulfill the desire of those who fear Him; He will also hear their cry and will save them.   *Psalm 145:18-19*

And in the same way the Spirit also helps our weakness; for we do not know how to pray as we should, but the Spirit Himself intercedes for *us* with groanings too deep for words; . . . .   *Romans 8:26*

Surely there is a future, And your hope will not be cut off.
                                                        Proverbs 23:18

Our steps are made firm by the Lord, when he delights in our way; though we stumble, we shall not fall headlong, for the Lord holds us by the hand.   *Psalm 37:23* (NRSV)

He brought me out of the pit of destruction, out of the miry clay; And He set my feet upon a rock making my footsteps firm.   *Psalm 40:2*

He raises the poor from the dust, And lifts the needy from the ash heap. To make *them* sit with princes, With the princes of His people.
                                                        Psalm 113:7-8

Then my enemies will turn back in the day when I call; This I Know, that God is for me.   *Psalm 56:9*

Who executes justice for the oppressed; Who gives food to the hungry. The Lord sets the prisoners free. The Lord opens *the eyes of* the blind; The Lord raises up those who are bowed down; The Lord loves the righteous; The Lord protects the strangers; He supports the fatherless and the widow; But He thwarts the way of the wicked.   *Psalm 146:7-9*

When my anxious thoughts multiply within me, Thy consolations delight my soul.   *Psalm 94:19*

"A bruised reed He will not break, And a dimly burning wick He will not extinguish; He will faithfully bring forth justice."   *Isaiah 42:3*

He sent from on high, He took me; He drew me out of many waters. He delivered me from my strong enemy, And from those who hated me, for they were too mighty for me. They confronted me in the day of my calamity, But the Lord was my stay. He brought me forth also into a broad place; He rescued me, because He delighted in me.
                                                          Psalm 18:16-19

Have you not known? Have you not heard? The Lord is the Everlasting God, the Creator of the ends of the earth. He does not faint or grow weary; his understanding is unsearchable. He gives power to the faint, and strengthens the powerless.   *Isaiah 40:28-29* (NRSV)

"You were tired out by the length of your road, *Yet* you did not say, 'It is hopeless.' You found renewed strength, Therefore you did not faint."
                                                          Isaiah 57:10

Restore to me the joy of Thy salvation, And sustain me with a willing spirit.   *Psalm 51:12*

Sustain me according to Thy word, that I may live; And do not let me be ashamed of my hope.   *Psalm 119:116*

"Come to Me, all who are weary and heavy-laden, and I will give you rest. Take My yoke upon you, and learn from Me, for I am gentle and humble in heart; and you shall find rest for your souls. For My yoke is easy, and My load is light."   *Matthew 11:28-30*

Mistrust

The fear of others lays a snare, but one who trusts in the Lord is secure.
Proverbs 29:25 (NRSV)

For thus the Lord God, the Holy One of Israel, has said, "In repentance and rest you shall be saved, In quietness and trust is your strength." But you were not willing, ...   *Isaiah 30:15*

Blessed are those who trust in the Lord, whose trust is the Lord. They shall be like a tree planted by the water, sending out its roots by the stream. It shall not fear when heat comes, and its leaves shall stay green; in the year of drought it is not anxious."   *Jeremiah 17:7-8* (NRSV)

Of Benjamin he said, "May the beloved of the Lord dwell in security by Him, Who shields him all the day, And he dwells between His shoulders."   *Deuteronomy 33:12*

The steps of a man are established by the Lord; And He delights in his way. When he falls, he shall not be hurled headlong; Because the Lord is the One who holds his hand.   *Psalm 37:24*

But as for me, I trust in Thee, O Lord, I say, "Thou art my God." My times are in Thy hand; Deliver me from the hand of my enemies, and from those who persecute me.   *Psalm 31:14-15*

All our steps are ordered by the Lord; how then can we understand our own ways?   *Proverbs 20:24* (NRSV)

"It will also come to pass that before they call, I will answer; and while they are still speaking, I will hear."   *Isaiah 65:24*

The Lord is near to all who call upon Him, To all who call upon Him in truth.   *Psalm 45:18*

And my God shall supply all your needs according to His riches in glory in Christ Jesus.   *Philippians 4:19*

". . . do not be anxious for your life, *as to* what you shall eat, or what you shall drink; nor for your body, *as to* what you shall put on. Is not life more than food, and the body than clothing? Look at the birds of the air, that they do not sow, neither do they reap, nor gather into barns, and *yet* your heavenly Father feeds them. Are you not worth much more than they? And which of you by being anxious can add a *single* cubit to his life's span? And why are you anxious about clothing? Observe how the lilies of the field grow; they do not toil nor do they spin, yet I say to you that even Solomon in all his glory did not clothe himself like one of these. But if God so arrays the grass of the field, which is *alive* today and tomorrow is thrown into the furnace, *will He* not much more *do so for* you — you of little faith? Do not be anxious then, saying, 'What shall we eat?' or 'What shall we drink?' or 'With what shall we clothe ourselves?' For all these things the Gentiles eagerly seek; for your heavenly Father knows that you need all these things. But seek first His kingdom and His righteousness; and all these things shall be added to you. Therefore do not be anxious for tomorrow; for tomorrow will care for itself. *Each* day has enough trouble of its own."   *Matthew 6:25-34*

"O Jerusalem, Jerusalem, who kills the prophets and stones those who are sent to her! How often I wanted to gather your childen together, the way a hen gathers her chicks under her wings, and you were unwilling."   *Matthew 23:37*

And He said to them, "Why are you troubled, and why do doubts arise in your hearts?"   *Luke 24:38*

And those who know Thy name will put their trust in Thee; For Thou, O Lord, hast not forsaken those who seek Thee.   *Psalm 9:10*

Happy are those who make the Lord their trust, who do not turn to the proud, to those who go astray after false gods.   *Psalm 40:4* (NRSV)

Woe to those who go down to Egypt for help, *And* rely on horses, And trust in chariots because they are many, And in horsemen because they are very strong, But they do not look to the Holy One of Israel, nor seek the Lord!   *Isaiah 31:1*

She heeded no voice; She accepted no instruction. She did not trust in the Lord; She did not draw near to her God.   *Zephaniah 3:2*

Trust in the Lord with all your heart, And do not lean on your own understanding. In all your ways acknowledge Him, And He will make your paths straight. Do not be wise in your own eyes; Fear the Lord and turn away from evil.   *Proverbs 3:5-7*

Temporary Relief

For I am confident of this very thing, that He who began a good work in you will perfect it until the day of Christ Jesus.   *Philippians 1:6*

"As for what was sown on rocky ground, this is the one who hears the word and immediately receives it with joy; yet such a person has no root, but endures only for a while, and then trouble or persecution arises on account of the word, that person immediately falls away.
                              Matthew 13:20-21 (NRSV)

There is a way that seems right to a person, but its end is the way to death.   *Proverbs 14:12* (NRSV)

Woe to those who go down to Egypt for help, *And* rely on horses, And trust in chariots because they are many, And in horsemen because they are very strong, But they do not look to the Holy One of Israel, nor seek the Lord! *Isaiah 31:1*

"Enter by the narrow gate; for the gate is wide, and the way is broad that leads to destruction, and many are those who enter by it. For the gate is small, and the way is narrow that leads to life, and few are those who find it." *Matthew 7:13-14*

By faith Moses, when he had grown up, refused to be called the son of Pharaoh's daughter; choosing rather to endure ill-treatment with the people of God, than to enjoy the passing pleasures of sin; . . . .
Hebrews 11:24-25

For here we do not have a lasting city, but we are seeking *the city* which is to come. *Hebrews 13:14*

Self-Pity

Where can I go from Thy Spirit? Or where can I flee from Thy presence? If I ascend to heaven, Thou art there; If I make my bed in Sheol, behold, Thou art there. If I take the wings of the dawn, If I dwell in the remotest part of the sea, Even there Thy hand will lead me, And Thy right hand will lay hold of me. If I say, "Surely the darkness will overwhelm me, And the light around me will be night," Even the darkness is not dark to Thee, And the night is as bright as the day. Darkness and light are alike *to Thee.* *Psalm 139:7-12*

Do not say, "Why is it that the former days were better than these?" For it is not from wisdom that you ask about this. *Ecclesiastes 7:10*

"You said, 'Ah, woe is me! For the Lord has added sorrow to my pain; I am weary with my groaning and have found no rest.' " *Jeremiah 45:3*

. . . in everything give thanks; for this is God's will for you in Christ Jesus.   *1 Thessalonians 5:18*

In this you greatly rejoice, even though now for a little while, if necessary, you have been distressed by various trials, that the proof of your faith, *being* more precious than gold which is perishable, even though tested by fire, may be found to result in praise and glory and honor at the revelation of Jesus Christ; . . . .   *1 Peter 1:7*

Why are you in despair, O my soul? And *why* have you become disturbed within me? Hope in God, for I shall again praise Him *For* the help of His presence.   *Psalm 42:5*

Behold, the Lord's hand is not so short That it cannot save; Neither is His ear so dull That it cannot hear.   *Isaiah 59:1*

Malicious witnesses rise up; They ask me of things that I do not know.
     Psalm 35:11

Lord, how long wilt Thou look on? Rescue my soul from their ravages, My only *life* from the lions.   *Psalm 35:17*

Do not fret because of evildoers, Be not envious toward wrongdoers. For they will wither quickly like the grass, And fade like the green herb.
     Psalm 37:1-2

No testing has overtaken you that is not common to everyone. God is faithful, and he will not let you be tested beyond your strength, but with the testing he will also provide the way out so that you may be able to endure it.   *1 Corinthians 10:13* (NRSV)

"Do not fear, you worm Jacob, . . . I will help you," declares the Lord, "and your Redeemer is the Holy One of Israel."   *Isaiah 41:14*

Woe is me, because of my injury! My wound is incurable. But I said, "Truly this is a sickness, And I must bear it."   *Jeremiah 10:19*

Then God said to Jonah, "Do you have good reason to be angry about the plant?" And he said, "I have good reason to be angry, even to death." Then the Lord said, "You had compassion on the plant for which you did not work, and *which* you did not cause to grow, which came up overnight and perished overnight. And should I not have compassion on Nineveh, the great city in which there are more than 120,000 persons who do not know *the difference* between their right and left hand, as well as many animals?"   *Jonah 4:9-11*

For consider Him who has endured such hostility by sinners against Himself, so that you may not grow weary and lose heart.   *Hebrews 12:4a*

Unworthiness

The Lord redeems the soul of His servants; And none of those who take refuge in Him will be condemned.   *Psalm 34:22*

Do not cast me away from Thy presence, And do not take Thy Holy Spirit from me.   *Psalm 51:11*

"The Spirit of the Lord is upon Me, Because He anointed Me to preach the gospel to the poor. He has sent Me to proclaim release to the captives, And recovery of sight to the blind, To set free those who are downtrodden. . . ."   *Luke 4:18*

Keep me as the apple of Thy eye; Hide me in the shadow of Thy wings, ...   *Psalm 17:8*

But you are a chosen race, a royal priesthood, a holy nation, a people for God's own possession, that you may proclaim the excellencies of Him Who has called you out of darkness into His marvelous light; . . . .   *1 Peter 2:9*

For He says to Moses, "I will have mercy on whom I have mercy, and I will have compassion on whom I have compassion." So it depends not on human will or exertion, but on God who shows mercy.

Romans 9:15-16 (NRSV)

For Thou didst form my inward parts; Thou didst weave me in my mother's womb. I will give thanks to Thee, for I am fearfully and wonderfully made; Wonderful are Thy works, And my soul knows it very well. My frame was not hidden from Thee, When I was made in secret, *And* skillfully wrought in the depths of the earth. Thine eyes have seen my unformed substance; And in Thy book they were all written, The days that were ordained *for me,* When as yet there was not one of them. How precious also are Thy thoughts to me, O God! How vast is the sum of them!   *Psalm 139:13-17*

For God has not destined us for wrath, but for obtaining salvation through our Lord Jesus Christ, ...   *1 Thessalonians 5:9*

The Lord is gracious and merciful; Slow to anger and great in loving-kindness. The Lord is good to all, And His mercies are over all His works.   *Psalm 145:8-9*

"And he who does not take his cross and follow after Me is not worthy of Me."   *Matthew 10:38*

For you did not receive a spirit of slavery to fall back into fear, but you have received a spirit of adoption. When we cry, "Abba! Father!" it is that very Spirit bearing witness with our spirit that we are children of God, and if children, then heirs, heirs of God and joint heirs with Christ — if, in fact, we suffer with him so that we may also be glorified with him.   *Romans 8:15-17*

And because you are children, God has sent the Spirit of His Son into our hearts, crying, "Abba! Father!" So you are no longer a slave but a child, and if a child then also an heir, through God.

Galatians 4:6 (NRSV)

Blessed is the nation whose God is the Lord, The people whom He has chosen for His own inheritance.   *Psalm 33:12*

You whom I have taken from the ends of the earth, And called from its remotest parts, And said to you, "You are My servant, I have chosen you and not rejected you."   *Isaiah 41:9*

Thus says the Lord who made you And formed you from the womb, who will help you, "Do not fear, O Jacob My servant; And you Jeshurun whom I have chosen."   *Isaiah 44:2*

"Do not be afraid, little flock, for your Father has chosen gladly to give you the kingdom."   *Luke 12:32*

And so, as those who have been chosen of God, holy and beloved, put on a heart of compassion, kindness, humility, gentleness and patience; . . . .
Colossians 3:12

But we must always give thanks to God for you, brothers and sisters beloved by the Lord, because God chose you as the first fruits for salvation through santification by the Spirit and through belief in the truth.
2 Thessalonians 2:13 (NRSV)

Fear

The fear of others lays a snare, but one who trusts in the Lord is secure.   *Proverbs 29:25* (NRSV)

"In righteousness you will be established; You will be far from oppression, for you will not fear; And from terror, for it will not come near you."   *Isaiah 54:14*

"And the Lord is the one who goes ahead of you; He will be with you. He will not fail you or forsake you. Do not fear, or be dismayed."

Deuteronomy 31:8

Thou didst draw near when I called on Thee; Thou didst say, "Do not fear!" O Lord, Thou didst plead my soul's cause; Thou hast redeemed my life.   *Lamentations 3:57-58*

"And he shall say to them, 'Hear, O Israel, you are approaching the battle against your enemies today. Do not be fainthearted. Do not be afraid, or panic, or tremble before them, for the Lord your God is the one who goes with you, to fight for you against your enemies, to save you.' "

Deuteronomy 20:3-4

I said to you, "Have no dread or fear of them. The Lord your God, who goes before you, is the one who will fight for you, just as he did for you in Egypt before your very eyes, and in the wilderness, where you saw how the Lord your God carried you, just as one carries a child, all the way that you traveled until you reached this place."

Deuteronomy 1:29-31 (NRSV)

For He has delivered me from all trouble; And my eye has looked *with satisfaction* upon my enemies.   *Psalm 54:7*

Even though I walk through the valley of the shadow of death, I fear no evil; for Thou art with me; Thy rod and Thy staff, they comfort me.

Psalm 23:4

Thou art my hiding place; Thou dost preserve me from trouble; Thou dost surround me with songs of deliverance.   *Psalm 32:7*

When I am afraid, I will put my trust in Thee. In God, whose word I praise, In God I have put my trust; I shall not be afraid. What can *mere* man do to me?   *Psalm 56:3-4*

God is our refuge and strength, A very present help in trouble. Therefore we will not fear, though the earth should change, And though the mountains slip into the heart of the sea; . . . .   *Psalm 46:1-2*

"Peace I leave with you; My peace I give to you; not as the world gives, do I give to you. Let not your heart be troubled, nor let it be fearful."
John 14:27

For you did not receive a spirit of slavery to fall back into fear, but you have received a spirit of adoption. When we cry, "Abba! Father!" . . . .   *Romans 8:15* (NRSV)

You will not be afraid of the terror by night, Or of the arrow that flies by day; Of the pestilence that stalks in darkness, Or of the destruction that lays waste at noon.   *Psalm 91:5-6*

For God has not given us a spirit of timidity, but of power and love and discipline.   *2 Timothy 1:7*

"No weapon that is formed against you shall prosper; And every tongue that accuses you in judgment you will condemn. This is the heritage of the servants of the Lord, And their vindication is from Me," declares the Lord.   *Isaiah 54:17*

"Have I not commanded you? Be strong and courageous! Do not tremble or be dismayed, for the Lord your God is with you wherever you go."
Joshua 1:9

When I saw *their fear,* I rose and spoke to the nobles, the officials, and the rest of the people: "Do not be afraid of them; remember the Lord who is great and awesome, and fight for your brothers, your sons, your daughters, your wives, and your houses."   *Nehemiah 4:14*

So he answered, "Do not fear, for those who are with us are more than those who are with them." *2 Kings 6:16*

The Lord is my light and my salvation; Whom shall I fear? The Lord is the defense of my life; Whom shall I dread? When evildoers came upon me to devour my flesh, My adversaries and my enemies, they stumbled and fell. Though a host encamp against me, My heart will not fear; Though war arise against me, In *spite of* this I shall be confident. One thing I have asked from the Lord, that I shall seek: That I may dwell in the house of the Lord all the days of my life, To behold the beauty of the Lord, And to meditate in His temple. For in the day of trouble He will conceal me in His tabernacle; In the secret place of His tent He will hide me; He will lift me up on a rock. *Psalm 27:1-5*

There is no fear in love; but perfect love casts out fear, because fear involves punishment, and the one who fears is not perfected in love.
1 John 4:18

But Thou, O Lord, art a shield about me, My glory, and the One who lifts my hand. I was crying to the Lord with my voice, And he answered me from His holy mountain. I lay down and slept; I awoke, for the Lord sustains me. I will not be afraid of ten thousands of people who have set themselves against me round about. *Psalm 3:3-6*

"Do not be afraid, little flock, for your Father has chosen gladly to give you the kingdom." *Luke 12:32*

Vengefulness

Never take your own revenge, beloved, but leave room for the wrath of God, for it is written, "Vengeance is Mine, I will repay," says the Lord. "But if your enemy is hungry, feed him, and if he is thirsty, give him a drink; for in so doing you will heap burning coals upon his head. Do not be overcome by evil, but overcome evil with good."
Romans 12:19-21

Do not say, "I will repay evil"; Wait for the Lord, and He will save you.
Proverbs 20:22

Do not rejoice when your enemy fails, and do not let your heart be glad when they stumble, or else the Lord will see it and be displeased, and turn away His anger from them.   *Proverbs 24:17-18* (NRSV)

At that time the disciples came to Jesus and asked, "Who is the greatest in the kingdom of heaven?" He called a child, whom he put among them, and said, "Truly I tell you, unless you change and become like children, you will never enter the kingdom of heaven. Whoever becomes humble like this child is the greatest in the kingdom of heaven. Whoever welcomes one such child in my name welcomes me.

If any of you put a stumbling block before one of these little ones who believe in me, it would be better for you if a great millstone were fastened around your neck and you were drowned in the depth of the sea. Woe to the world because of stumbling blocks! Occasions for stumbling are bound to come, but woe to the one by whom the stumbling block comes!

If your hand or your foot causes you to stumble, cut it off and throw it away; it is better for you to enter life maimed or lame than to have two hands or two feet and to be thrown into the eternal fire. And if your eye causes you to stumble, tear it out and throw it away; it is better for you to enter life with one eye than to have two eyes and to be thrown into the hell of fire.

Take care that you do not despise one of these little ones; for, I tell you, in heaven their angels continually see the face of my Father in heaven."   *Matthew 18:1-11* (NRSV)

You shall not hate in your heart anyone of your kin; you shall reprove your neighbor, or you will incur guilt yourself. You shall not take vengeance or bear a grudge against any of your people, but you shall love your neighbor as yourself; I am the Lord.   *Leviticus 19:17-18* (NRSV)

"Vengeance is Mine, and retribution, In due time their foot will slip; For the day of their calamity is near, And the impending things are hastening upon them."   *Deuteronomy 32:35*

Say to those with anxious heart, "Take courage, fear not. Behold, your God will come *with* vengeance; The recompense of God will come, But He will save you."   *Isaiah 35:4*

But, O Lord of hosts, who judges righteously, Who tries the feelings and the heart, Let me see Thy vengeance on them, For to Thee have I committed my cause.   *Jeremiah 11:20*

Thou who knowest, O Lord, Remember me, take notice of me, And take vengeance for me on my persecutors. Do *not,* in view of Thy patience, take me away; Know that for Thy sake I endure reproach.
Jeremiah 15:15

Therefore thus says the Lord, "Behold, I am going to plead your case And exact full vengeance for you; And I shall dry up her sea And make her fountain dry."   *Jeremiah 51:36*

Remember my affliction and my wandering, the wormwood and bitterness.   *Lamentations 3:19*

See to it that no one comes short of the grace of God; that no root of bitterness springing up causes trouble, and by it many be defiled; . . . .
Hebrews 12:15

Then the Lord knows how to rescue the godly from temptation, and to keep the unrighteous under punishment for the day of judgment.
2 Peter 2:9

HEALING **JOURNAL**
leg 21 / discouragement

Use this page to record your personal thoughts and reflections.

leg 21 / discouragement

Use this page to record your special Bible verses that encourage you on the journey (verses need not be limited to the ones in this book).

HEALING **JOURNAL**
leg 22 / pride

Use this page to record your personal thoughts and reflections.

leg 22 / pride

Use this page to record your special Bible verses that encourage you on the journey (verses need not be limited to the ones in this book).

HEALING **JOURNAL**
leg 23 / compromise

Use this page to record your personal thoughts and reflections.

leg 23 / compromise

Use this page to record your special Bible verses that encourage you on the journey (verses need not be limited to the ones in this book).

HEALING **JOURNAL**
leg 24 / aimlessness

Use this page to record your personal thoughts and reflections.

leg 24 / aimlessness

Use this page to record your special Bible verses that encourage you on the journey (verses need not be limited to the ones in this book).

HEALING **JOURNAL**
leg 25 / ridicule

Use this page to record your personal thoughts and reflections.

leg 25 / ridicule

Use this page to record your special Bible verses that encourage you on the journey (verses need not be limited to the ones in this book).

HEALING **JOURNAL**
leg 26 / rejection

Use this page to record your personal thoughts and reflections.

leg 26 / rejection

Use this page to record your special Bible verses that encourage you on the journey (verses need not be limited to the ones in this book).

HEALING **JOURNAL**
leg 27 / unbelief

Use this page to record your personal thoughts and reflections.

leg 27 / unbelief

Use this page to record your special Bible verses that encourage you on the journey (verses need not be limited to the ones in this book).

HEALING **JOURNAL**
leg 28 / impatience

Use this page to record your personal thoughts and reflections.

leg 29 / hopelessness

Use this page to record your special Bible verses that encourage you on the journey (verses need not be limited to the ones in this book).

HEALING **JOURNAL**
leg 30 / mistrust

Use this page to record your personal thoughts and reflections.

leg 30 / mistrust

Use this page to record your special Bible verses that encourage you on the journey (verses need not be limited to the ones in this book).

HEALING **JOURNAL**
leg 31 / temporary relief

Use this page to record your personal thoughts and reflections.

leg 31 / temporary relief

Use this page to record your special Bible verses that encourage you on the journey (verses need not be limited to the ones in this book).

HEALING **JOURNAL**
leg 32 / self-pity

Use this page to record your personal thoughts and reflections.

leg 32 / self-pity

Use this page to record your special Bible verses that encourage you on the journey (verses need not be limited to the ones in this book).

HEALING **JOURNAL**
leg 33 / unworthiness

Use this page to record your personal thoughts and reflections.

just can't go back, no matter how rugged the trail might be."

Some survivors discover a new creativity never before experienced. Others describe a new ability to feel and to be genuinely sensitive to their surroundings.

One young man said, "Nature is becoming a wondrous adventure to me. It is as if my senses have come to life. Colors are more vibrant, smells more stimulating, and sounds draw my attention as never before. It's like a new beginning. Isn't God gracious to give us so many new beginnings?"

He went on to say that he still had problems in his daily life, but in spite of them, he felt released. It was as if God had brought him out into a broader place and gave him new wisdom and understanding.

Yet another survivor in her late twenties described her new response as one that makes you feel like a young colt set free to run in a beautiful open meadow.

After the feelings begin to move toward restoration, you begin to yearn for a sense of personal purpose. This longing has previously been a considerable dilemma for the victim of early abuse, especially if there has been no release from the inner confusion that accompanies the trauma of the past.

A need for purpose is a life-changing force: Knowing who you were made to be, and what you are called to do, produces not only emotional release but also a new and healthier response in your relationship to God. You were neither created to be a passive nor an overachieving victim who has no balance with which to measure success or failure.

You were created to fill a distinct purpose emotionally and spiritually as you respond to God, yourself, and others. Tearing down walls of woundedness can release you to begin the discovery of your own unique destiny and personhood. As the old patterns of dysfunction fall by the wayside, they are replaced by the truth of who you really are in Christ Jesus. Your purpose in Him starts to unfold. The glorious truth that you were made to be with Him in this life and for eternity becomes more real with every step of growth. Though one can't describe with total accuracy a dwelling that has never been seen, the Bible does give the hope and even assurance of Heaven to the one who reaches out for Jesus.

To travel the journey to emotional freedom from past hurts requires boundless courage. You are seeking our Lord, not just for the ultimate reward to spend eternity in God's kingdom, Heaven, but also for the expression of Heaven in this life. When you face and release the inner battles, the ensuing wholeness makes you more Christlike.

He begins to radiate through your genuine responses to life situations and relationships. Denial is no longer needed for survival. You become more at peace in every area of life. There is a newfound ability to be "in this world" (honestly facing humanity, including self) and yet not "of this world." Such a liberation begins to reveal a taste of Heaven to those about you. *You were created to love.* You were called to love God, others, and yourself in a healthy way. As you heal, all these expressions become more possible. Even your ability to receive love will be transformed.

Scripture shares that Heaven is the ultimate reward for those who trust Jesus. That is a real hope and point of faith for each believer. However, the kingdom of God is also in this world through hearts that are being purified to reflect Jesus.

There is more room for the Spirit of God to purify and teach you as your past hurts are exposed, felt, and released. Genuine intimacy is born out of real love. There are few areas as damaged by the distortions of your early victimization as the capacity to express pure intimate love in relationships. Such a love is critical in response to our Lord's command:

> "You shall love the Lord your God with all your heart and with all your soul, and with all your mind. This is the great and foremost commandment. And the second is like it, you shall love your neighbor as yourself."   *Matthew 22:37-39*

Intimacy, then, is a deep capacity to experience and express true love. You are called to this healthy love on two levels: You are to learn to love God with every fiber of your being, *and* you are called to love your neighbor with the same love that you extend to yourself.

Tragically, many victims see God through the distorted eyes of a child looking up at a perpetrator. He is just one more authority figure waiting to hurt them.

The victim may harbor such *self-condemnation* and hatred that to love others in such a manner might destroy them. What a dilemma! How can someone so hurt answer the call to love? The answer lies in a willingness to embark on the road to recovery. Because of your desire to become whole, even as God is whole, out of wholeness pure love will abound.

For many of you a trip back must be made — a search for the old wounds and a chance to remove the scar tissue that has blocked your healing.

Perhaps you will come face to face with Him in Heaven before you realize the fruit of facing yourself and your past. But this one thing you will know: Letting go of what lies behind has freed your heart at last to reach forward to what lies ahead.

The call to love has finally broken through the confusion of all your yesterdays. You are free to go on and grow as never before. Will you feel more pain in your present circumstances? Possibly. Now that your emotions are restored, you may be more sensitive to pain and any number of feelings. Don't be discouraged, for the other side of this new sensitivity is the ability to feel genuine joy and to love more deeply with greater capacity, purity, and intimacy.

You are accepting your humanity while preparing for eternity. Praise God, you are becoming complete in Him. Your journey through darkness ultimately leads to the dawn. The final design of such a darkness asks that we fall through it into His everlasting arms. As you cross over the bridge from victim to victor, you will look back at the miraculous work our God has done in your heart. Then you may find, as have so many others, that the darkness you have experienced on your journey is not the enemy of faith . . . but its friend.

Now as you travel the path to liberation, may the good hand of our God be upon you. May the light of our Lord Jesus Christ anoint and bless your every step as He restores the ancient ruins of your heart. And may He find for Himself a renewed dwelling place within you where His Spirit can teach you His gentle song of love.

Then I became in his eyes as one who finds peace.

And he is wholly desirable.
This is my beloved
and
this is my friend.

Song of Solomon 8:10b, 5:16b

Purpose

The Lord will accomplish what concerns me; Thy lovingkindness, O Lord, is everlasting; Do not forsake the works of Thy hands.

Psalm 138:8

The human mind plans the way, but the Lord directs the steps.

Proverbs 16:9 (NRSV)

"I know that Thou canst do all things, And that no purpose of Thine can be thwarted." *Job 42:2*

Now He who prepared us for this very purpose is God, who gave to us the Spirit as a pledge. *2 Corinthians 5:5*

It was for freedom that Christ set us free; therefore keep standing firm and do not be subject again to a yoke of slavery. *Galatians 5:1*

Therefore, since we have so great a cloud of witnesses surrounding us, let us also lay aside every encumbrance, and the sin which so easily entangles us, and let us run with endurance the race that is set before us, fixing our eyes on Jesus, the author and perfecter of faith, who for the joy set before Him endured the cross, despising the shame, and has set down at the right hand of the throne of God. *Hebrews 12:1-2*

The Lord is the portion of my inheritance and my cup; Thou dost support my lot. The lines have fallen to me in pleasant places; Indeed, my heritage is beautiful to me. *Psalm 16:5-6*

Therefore, thus says the Lord, "If you return, then I will restore you — Before Me you will stand; And if you extract the precious from the worthless, You will become My spokesman. They for their part may turn to you, But as for you, you must not turn to them." *Jeremiah 15:19*

He brought me up out of the pit of destruction, out of the miry clay; And He set my feet upon a rock making my footsteps firm. *Psalm 40:2*

"Blessed are those who trust in the Lord, whose trust is the Lord. They shall be like a tree planted by water, sending out its roots by the stream. It shall not fear when heat comes, and its leaves shall stay green: in the

year of drought it is not anxious, and it does not cease to bear fruit."
Jeremiah 17:7-8

Come *and* hear, all who fear God, And I will tell of what He has done for my soul.   *Psalm 66:16*

For we are His workmanship, created in Christ Jesus for good works, which God prepared beforehand, that we should walk in them.
Ephesians 2:10

Bear one another's burdens, and thus fulfill the law of Christ.
Galatians 6:2

So then, while we have opportunity, let us do good to all men, and especially to those who are of the household of the faith.   *Galatians 6:10*

Declaring the end from the beginning And from ancient times things which have not been done, Saying, "My purpose will be established, And I will accomplish all My good pleasure"; . . . .   *Isaiah 46:10*

And we know that God causes all things to work together for good to those who love God, to those who are called according to *His* purpose.   *Romans 8:28*

. . . also we have obtained an inheritance, having been predestined according to His purpose who works all things after the counsel of His will, ...   *Ephesians 1:11*

. . . make my joy complete by being of the same mind, maintaining the same love, united in spirit, intent on one purpose.   *Philippians 2:2*

For God has not called us for the purpose of impurity, but in sanctification.   *1 Thessalonians 4:7*

. . . who has saved us, and called us with a holy calling, not according to our works, but according to His own purpose and grace which was granted us in Christ Jesus from all eternity, ...   *2 Timothy 1:9*

For you have been called for this purpose, since Christ also suffered for you, leaving you an example for you to follow in His steps, ...

1 Peter 2:21

Therefore, since Christ has suffered in the flesh, arm yourselves also with the same purpose, because he who has suffered in the flesh has ceased from sin, ...   *1 Peter 4:1*

And Jesus came up and spoke to them, saying, "All authority has been given to Me in heaven and on earth. Go therefore and make disciples of all the nations, baptizing them in the name of the Father and the Son and the Holy Spirit, teaching them to observe all that I commanded you; and lo, I am with you always, even to the end of the age."

Matthew 28:18-20

Now the God of peace, . . . equip you in every good thing to do His will, working in us that which is pleasing in His sight, through Jesus Christ, to whom *be* the glory forever and ever. Amen.   *Hebrews 13:20a, 21*

Renewed Vitality

In the morning, O Lord, Thou wilt hear my voice; In the morning I will order *my prayer* to Thee and *eagerly* watch.   *Psalm 5:3*

"My very own vineyard is at my disposal;" . . . .

Song of Solomon 8:12a

By wisdom a house is built, And by understanding it is established; And by knowledge the rooms are filled With all precious and pleasant riches.

Proverbs 24:3-4

Bless the Lord, O my soul, And forget none of His benefits; Who pardons all your iniquities; Who heals all our diseases; Who redeems your life from the pit; Who crowns you with lovingkindness and compassion; Who satisfies your years with good things, *So that* your youth is renewed like the eagle.   *Psalm 103:2-5*

They will still yield fruit in old age; They shall be full of sap and very green, ...   *Psalm 92:14*

"Therefore you too now have sorrow; but I will see you again, and your heart will rejoice, and no one takes your joy away from you."
John 16:22

"Therefore, behold, I will allure her, Bring her into the wilderness, And speak kindly to her. Then I will give her her vineyards from there, And the valley of Achor as a door of hope. And she will sing there as in the days of her youth, As in the day when she came up from the land of Egypt."   *Hosea 2:14-15*

And the Lord restored the fortunes of Job when he prayed for his friends, and the Lord increased all that Job had twofold . . . And the Lord blessed the latter *days* of Job more than his beginning, . . . And he had seven sons and three daughters.   *Job 42:10, 12-13*

"Do not call to mind the former things, Or ponder things of the past. Behold, I will do something new, Now it will spring forth; Will you not be aware of it? I will even make a roadway in the wilderness. Rivers in the desert. The beasts of the field will glorify Me; The jackals and the ostriches; Because I have given waters in the wilderness And rivers in the desert. To give drink to My chosen people. The people whom I formed for Myself, Will declare My praise.   *Isaiah 43:18-21*

The point is this: the one who sows sparingly will reap sparingly, and the one who sows bountifully will also reap bountifully. Each of you must give as you have made up your mind, not reluctantly or under compulsion, for God loves a cheerful giver. And God is able to provide you with every blessing in abundance, so that by always having enough of everything, you may share abundantly in every good work.

2 Corinthians 9:6-8 (NRSV)

"And those from among you will rebuild the ancient ruins; You will raise up the age-old foundations; And you will be called the repairer of the breach, The restorer of the streets in which to dwell."   *Isaiah 58:12*

The Spirit of the Lord God is upon me, Because the Lord has anointed me To bring good news to the afflicted; He has sent me to bind up the broken-hearted, To proclaim liberty to captives, And freedom to prisoners;....

Isaiah 61:1

"Moreover, I will give you a new heart and put a new spirit within you; and I will remove the heart of stone from your flesh and give you a heart of flesh."   *Ezekiel 36:26*

When the Lord brought back the captive ones of Zion, We were like those who dream. Then our mouth was filled with laughter, And our tongue with joyful shouting; Then they said among the nations, "The Lord has done great things for them." The Lord has done great things for us; We are glad.   *Psalm 126:1-3*

And the ransomed of the Lord will return, And come with joyful shouting to Zion, With everlasting joy upon their heads. They will find gladness and joy, And sorrow and sighing will flee away.   *Isaiah 35:10*

The Spirit of the Lord God is upon me, Because the Lord has anointed me To bring good news to the afflicted; He has sent me to bind up the brokenhearted, To proclaim liberty to captives, And freedom to prisoners; To proclaim the favorable year of the Lord, And the day of vengeance of our God; To comfort all who mourn, To grant those who mourn *in* Zion, Giving them a garland instead of ashes, The oil of gladness instead of mourning, The mantle of praise instead of a spirit of fainting. So they will be called oaks of righteousness, The planting of the Lord, that He may be glorified. Then they will rebuild the ancient ruins,

They will raise up the former devastations, And they will repair the ruined cities, The desolations of many generations.   *Isaiah 61:1-4*

Intimacy

With Jesus:

So the ransomed of the Lord will return, And come with joyful shouting to Zion; And everlasting joy *will be* on their heads. They will obtain gladness and joy, And sorrow and sighing will flee away.   *Isaiah 51:11*

And we know that God causes all things to work together for good to those who love God, to those who are called according to *His* purpose.
Romans 8:28

"Sanctify them in the truth; Thy word is truth . . . And for their sakes I sanctify Myself, that they themselves also may be sanctified in truth . . . That they may all be one; even as Thou, Father, *art* in Me, and I in Thee, that they also may be in Us; that the world may believe that Thou didst send Me."   *John 17:17, 19, 21*

Surely goodness and lovingkindness will follow me all the days of my life, And I will dwell in the house of the Lord forever.   *Psalm 23:6*

One thing I have asked from the Lord, that I shall seek: That I may dwell in the house of the Lord all the days of my life, To behold the beauty of the Lord, And to meditate in His temple. For in the day of trouble He will conceal me in His tabernacle; In the secret place of His tent He will hide me; He will lift me up on a rock. And now my head will be lifted up above my enemies around me; And I will offer in His tent sacrifices with shouts of joy; I will sing, yes, I will sing praises to the Lord.
Psalm 27:4-6

But whatever things were gain to me, those things I have counted as loss for the sake of Christ. More than that, I count all things to be loss in view of the surpassing value of knowing Christ Jesus my Lord, for whom I have suffered the loss of all things, and count them but rubbish in order that I may gain Christ, . . . and may be found in Him, not having a right-eousness of my own derived from *the* Law, but that which is through faith in Christ, the righteousness which *comes* from God on the basis of faith, that I may know Him, and the power of His resurrection and the fellowship of His sufferings, being conformed to His death; in order that I may attain to the resurrection from the dead.   *Philippians 3:7-11*

Beloved, now we are children of God, and it has not appeared as yet what we shall be. We know that, when He appears, we shall be like Him, because we shall see Him just as He is.   *1 John 3:2*

Of Benjamin he said, "May the beloved of the Lord dwell in security by Him, Who shields him all the day, And he dwells between His shoulders."
Deuteronomy 33:12

"For behold, the winter is past, The rain is over *and* gone. The flowers have *already* appeared in the Land; The time has arrived for pruning *the vines,* And the voice of the turtledove has been heard in our land."
Song of Solomon 2:11-12

. . . and though you have not seen Him, you love Him, and though you do not see Him now, but believe in Him, you greatly rejoice with joy in-expressible and full of glory, obtaining as the outcome of your faith the salvation of your souls.   *1 Peter 1:8-9*

When I remember Thee on my bed, I meditate on Thee in the night watches, For Thou hast been my help, And in the shadow of Thy wings I sing for joy. My soul clings to Thee; Thy right hand upholds me.
Psalm 63:6-8

Nevertheless I am continually with Thee; Thou has taken hold of my right hand.   *Psalm 73:23*

. . . "And he is wholly desirable. This is my beloved and this is my friend," . . . . *Song of Solomon 5:16*

I appeal to you therefore, brothers and sisters, by the mercies of God, to present your bodies as a living sacrifice, holy and acceptable to God, which is your spiritual worship. *Romans 12:1* (NRSV)

"I have been crucified with Christ; and it is no longer I who live, but Christ lives in me; and the *life* which I now live in the flesh I live by faith in the Son of God, who loved me, and delivered Himself up for me."
Galatians 2:20

. . . "I will put My laws into their minds, And I will write them upon their hearts. And I will be their God, And they shall be My people."
Hebrews 8:10

"Now therefore, I pray Thee, if I have found favor in Thy sight, let me know Thy ways, that I may know Thee, so that I may find favor in Thy sight. Consider too, that this nation is Thy people." *Exodus 33:13*

"Just as the Father has loved Me, I have also loved you; abide in My love." *John 15:9*

"Greater love has no one than this, that one lay down his life for his friends." *John 15:13*

"No longer do I call you slaves, for the slave does not know what his master is doing; but I have called you friends, for all things that I have heard from My Father I have made known to you." *John 15:15*

"For God so loved the world, that He gave His only begotten Son, that whoever believes in Him should not perish, but have eternal life."
John 3:16

"He pled the cause of the afflicted and needy; Then it was well. Is not that what it means to know Me?" Declares the Lord. *Jeremiah 22:16*

"Now therefore, I pray Thee, if I have found favor in Thy sight, let me know Thy ways, that I may know Thee, so that I may find favor in Thy sight. Consider too, that this nation is Thy people." And He said, "My presence shall go *with you,* and I will give you rest."

Exodus 33:13-14

I pray that, according to the riches of his glory, he may grant that you may be strengthened in your inner being with power through his Spirit, and that Christ may dwell in your hearts through faith, as you are being rooted and grounded in love. I pray that you may have the power to comprehend, with all the saints, what is the breadth and length and height and depth, and to know the love of Christ that surpasses knowledge, so that you may be filled with all the fullness of God.

Ephesians 3:16-20 (NRSV)

"When the Son of Man comes in his glory, and all the angels with him, then he will sit on the throne of his glory. All the nations will be gathered before him; and he will separate people one from another as the shepherd separates the sheep from the goats, and he will put the sheep on his right, and the goats on the left. Then the King will say to those on his right hand 'Come, you who are blessed by my Father, inherit the kingdom prepared for you from the foundation of the world; for I was hungry, and you gave me food, I was thirsty, and you gave me something to drink; I was a stranger, and you welcomed me, I was naked and you gave me clothing, I was sick and you took care of me, I was in prison and you visited me.' Then the righteous will answer him, 'Lord, when was it that we saw you hungry and gave you food, or thirsty and gave you something to drink? And when was it that we saw you a stranger and welcomed you, or naked and gave you clothing? And when was it that we saw you sick or in prison and visited you?' And the king will answer them, 'Truly I tell you, just as you did it to one of the least of these who are members of my family, you did it to me.' " *Matthew 25:31-40* (NRSV)

Faithful is He who calls you, and He also will bring it to pass.

1 Thessalonians 5:24

And may the Lord direct your hearts into the love of God and into the steadfastness of Christ.   *2 Thessalonians 3:5*

With Others:

If then there is any encouragement in Christ, any consolation from love, any sharing in the Spirit, any compassion and sympathy, make my joy complete: be of the same mind, having the same love, being in full accord and of one mind. Do nothing from selfish ambition or conceit, but in humility regard others as better than yourselves. Let each of you look not to your own interests, but to the interests of others.

Philippians 2:1-4 (NRSV)

"Therefore, however you want people to treat you, so treat them, for this is the Law and the Prophets."   *Matthew 7:12*

Those who are taught the word must share in all good things with their teacher.   *Galatians 6:6 (NRSV)*

So then, whenever we have an opportunity, let us work for the good of all, and especially for those of the family of faith.

Galatians 6:10 (NRSV)

. . . that no one wrong or exploit a brother or sister in this matter, because the Lord is an avenger in all these things, just as we have already told you beforehand and solemnly warned you.

1 Thessalonians 4:6 (NRSV)

Therefore encourage one another and build up each other, as indeed you are doing. But we appeal to you, brothers and sisters, to respect those who labor among you, and have charge of you in the Lord and admonish you; esteem them very highly in love because of their work.

1 Thessalonians 5:11-13 (NRSV)

Let mutual love continue. Do not neglect to show hospitality to strangers, for by doing that some have entertained angels without knowing it. *Hebrews 13:1-2* (NRSV)

Finally, brothers and sisters, farewell. Put things in order, listen to my appeal, agree with one another, live in peace; and the God of love and peace will be with you. *2 Corinthians 13:11* (NRSV)

See that none of you repays evil for evil, but always seek to do good to one another and to all. *1 Thessalonians 5:15* (NRSV)

I thank my God in all my remembrance of you, always offering prayer with joy in my every prayer for you all, in view of your participation in the gospel from the first day until now. *For I am* confident of this very thing, that He who began a good work in you will perfect it until the day of Christ Jesus. For it is only right for me to feel this way about you all, because I have you in my heart, since both in my imprisonment and in the defense and confirmation of the gospel, you all are partakers of grace with me. For God is my witness, how I long for you all with the affection of Christ Jesus. *Philippians 1:3-8*

And let the peace of Christ rule in your hearts, to which indeed you were called in one body; and be thankful. *Colossians 3:15*

And they were continually devoting themselves to the apostles' teaching and to fellowship, to the breaking of bread and to prayer. *Acts 2:42*

Now may the God who gives perseverance and encouragement grant you to be of the same mind with one another according to Christ Jesus; that with one accord you may with one voice glorify the God and Father of our Lord Jesus Christ. *Romans 15:5-6*

For I long to see you in order that I may impart some spiritual gift to you, that you may be established; . . . I may be encouraged together with you *while* among you, each of us by the other's faith, both yours and mine. *Romans 1:11-12*

We must no longer be children, tossed to and fro and blown about by every wind of doctrine, by people's trickery, by their craftiness in deceitful scheming. But speaking the truth in love, we must grow up in every way into him who is the head, into Christ, from whom the whole body, joined and knit together by every ligament with which it is equipped, as each part is working properly, promotes the body's growth in building itself up in love.   *Ephesians 4:14-16* (NRSV)

. . . love one another with mutual affection; outdo one another in showing honor. Do not lag in zeal, be ardent in spirit, serve the Lord. Rejoice in hope, be patient in suffering, persevere in prayer. Contribute to the needs of the saints; extend hospitality to strangers.

Bless those who persecute you; bless and do not curse them. Rejoice with those who rejoice, weep with those who weep. Live in harmony with one another; do not be haughty, but associate with the lowly; do not claim to be wiser than you are. Do not repay anyone evil for evil, but take thought for what is noble in the sight of all. If it is possible, so far as it depends on you, live peaceably with all.   *Romans 12:10-18* (NRSV)

Above all, keep fervent in your love for one another, because love covers a multitude of sins.   *1 Peter 4:8*

Let all bitterness and wrath and anger and clamor and slander be put away from you, along with all malice. And be kind to one another, tender-hearted, forgiving each other, just as God in Christ also has forgiven you.   *Ephesians 4:31-32*

For this is the message which you have heard from the beginning, that we should love one another; Little children, let us not love with word or with tongue, but in deed and truth.   *1 John 3:11, 18*

Beloved, let us love one another, for love is from God; and everyone who loves is born of God and knows God. The one who does not love does not know God, for God is love. By this the love of God was manifested in us, that God has sent His only begotten Son into the world so that we might live through Him. In this is love, not that we loved God, but that He loved us and sent His Son *to be* the propitiation for our sins. Beloved, if God so loved us, we also ought to love one another. No one has beheld God at any time; if we love one another, God abides in us, and His love is perfected in us.　　*1 John 4:7-12*

With Ourselves:

And he answered and said, "You shall love the Lord your God with all your heart, and with all your soul, and with all your strength, and with all your mind; and your neighbor as yourself."　　*Luke 10:27*

Rejoice always; pray without ceasing; in everything give thanks; for this is God's will for you in Christ Jesus.　　*1 Thessalonians 5:16-18*

We are destroying speculations and every lofty thing raised up against the knowledge of God, and *we are* taking every thought captive to the obedience of Christ, ...　　*2 Corinthians 10:5*

For the whole Law is fulfilled in one word, in the *statement,* "You shall love your neighbor as yourself."　　*Galatians 5:14*

If, however, you are fulfilling the royal law, according to the Scripture, "You shall love your neighbor as yourself," you are doing well.
　　　　　　　　　　　　　　　　　　　　　　　　James 2:8

And this I pray, that your love may abound still more and more in real knowledge and all discernment, . . . so that you may approve the things that are excellent, in order to be sincere and blameless until the day of Christ;　　*Philippians 1:9-10*

We love, because He first loved us.　　*1 John 4:19*

For we through the Spirit, by faith, are waiting for the hope of righteousness. For in Christ Jesus neither circumcision nor uncircumcision means anything, but faith working through love.   *Galatians 5:5-6*

All things are lawful for me, but not all things are profitable. All things are lawful for me, but I will not be mastered by anything. Food is for the stomach, and the stomach is for food; but God will do away with both of them. Yet the body is not for immortality, but for the Lord; and the Lord is for the body.   *1 Corinthians 6:12-13*

(For the fruit of the light *consists* in all goodness and righteousness and truth), trying to learn what is pleasing to the Lord.   *Ephesians 5:9-10*

Do all things without grumbling or disputing; that you may prove yourselves to be blameless and innocent, children of God above reproach in the midst of a crooked and perverse generation, among whom you appear as lights in the world, ...   *Philippians 2:14-15*

But whatever things were gain to me, those things I have counted as loss for the sake of Christ. . . . that I may know Him, and the power of His resurrection and the fellowship of His sufferings, being conformed to His death; . . . .   *Philippians 3:7, 10*

Let your gentleness be known to everyone. The Lord is near.
Philippians 4:5a (NRSV)

Not that I speak from want; for I have learned to be content in whatever circumstances I am. . . . I can do all things through Him who strengthens me.   *Philippians 4:11, 13*

Let the word of Christ richly dwell within you, with all wisdom teaching and admonishing one another with psalms *and* hymns *and* spiritual songs, singing with thankfulness in your hearts to God.
Colossians 3:16

Whatever your task, put yourselves into it, as done for the Lord and not for your masters, since you know that from the Lord you will receive the inheritance as your reward; you serve the Lord Christ.

Colossians 3:23-24 (NRSV)

But examine everything *carefully*; hold fast to that which is good; . . . .

1 Thessalonians 5:21

He has told you, . . . what is good; And what does the Lord require of you, but to do justice, to love kindness, and to walk humbly with your God?   *Micah 6:8*

Brothers and sisters, do not grow weary of doing good.

2 Thessalonians 3:13

When Jesus saw the crowds, he went up the mountain; and after he sat down, his disciples came to him. Then he began to speak, and taught them, saying; "Blessed are the poor in spirit, for theirs is the kingdom of heaven. Blessed are those who mourn, for they will be comforted. Blessed are the meek, for they will inherit the earth. Blessed are those who hunger and thirst for righteousness, for they will be filled. Blessed are the merciful, for they will receive mercy. Blessed are the pure in heart, for they will see God. Blessed are the peacemakers, for they will be called children of God. Blessed are those who are persecuted for right-eousness' sake, for theirs is the kingdom of heaven. Blessed are you when people revile you and persecute you and utter all kinds of evil against you falsely on my account. Rejoice and be glad, for your reward is great in heaven, for in the same way they persecuted the prophets who were before you."   *Matthew 5:1-12* (NRSV)

Peace

The Lord's lovingkindnesses indeed never cease, For His compassions never fail. *They* are new every morning; Great is Thy faithfulness.

Lamentations 3:22-23

. . . Then I became in his eyes as one who finds peace.
Song of Solomon 8:10

The things you have learned and received and heard and seen in me, practice these things; and the God of peace shall be with you.
Philippians 4:9

"Behold, I will bring to it health and healing, and I will heal them; and I will reveal to them an abundance of peace and truth."   *Jeremiah 33:6*

A tranquil heart is life to the body, ...   *Proverbs 14:30*

When the ways of people please the Lord, he causes even their enemies to be at peace with them.   *Proverbs 16:7* (NRSV)

Return to your rest, O my soul, For the Lord has dealt bountifully with you.   *Psalm 116:7*

Now may the God of hope fill you with all joy and peace in believing, that you may abound in hope by the power of the Holy Spirit.
Romans 15:13

And the peace of God, which surpasses all comprehension, shall guard your hearts and your minds in Christ Jesus.   *Philippians 4:7*

Now may the Lord of peace Himself continually grant you peace in every circumstance. The Lord be with you all!   *2 Thessalonians 3:16*

How beautiful upon the mountains are the feet of the messenger who announces peace, who brings good news, ...   *Isaiah 52:7* (NRSV)

Those who love Thy law have great peace, And nothing causes them to stumble.   *Psalm 119:165*

"Peace I leave with you; My peace I give to you; not as the world gives, do I give to you. Let not your heart be troubled, nor let it be fearful."
John 14:27

In peace I will both lie down and sleep, For Thou alone, O Lord, dost make me to dwell in safety.   *Psalm 4:8*

The Lord will give strength to His people; The Lord will bless His people with peace.   *Psalm 29:11*

He will redeem my soul in peace from the battle *which is* against me, For they are many *who strive* with me.   *Psalm 55:18*

"The steadfast of mind Thou wilt keep in perfect peace, Because he trusts in Thee."   *Isaiah 26:3*

And the work of righteousness will be peace, And the service of righteousness, quietness and confidence forever.   *Isaiah 32:17*

"For the mountains may be removed and the hills may shake, But My lovingkindness will not be removed from you, And My covenant of peace will not be shaken," Says the Lord who has compassion on you.
Isaiah 54:10

Peace, peace, to the far and the near, says the Lord; and I will heal them.
Isaiah 57:19 (NRSV)

"These things I have spoken to you, that in Me you may have peace. In the world you have tribulation; but take courage; I have overcome the world."   *John 16:33*

For the mind set on the flesh is death, but the mind set on the Spirit is life and peace, ...   *Romans 8:6*

But the fruit of the spirit is love, joy, peace, patience, kindness, goodness, faithfulness, ...   *Galatians 5:22*

. . . And the peace of God, which surpasses all comprehension, shall
guard your hearts and your minds in Christ Jesus.   *Philippians 4:7*

Heaven

"Let not your heart be troubled; believe in God, believe also in Me. In
My Father's house are many dwelling places; if it were not so, I would
have told you; for I go to prepare a place for you. And if I go and prepare a place for you, I will come again, and receive you to Myself; that
where I am, *there* you may be also.   *John 14:1-3*

"Rejoice, and be glad, for your reward in heaven is great, ...
    Matthew 5:12

At that time the disciples came to Jesus and asked, "Who is the greatest
in the kingdom of heaven?" He called a child, whom he put among
them, and said, "Truly I tell you, unless you change and become like
children, you will never enter the kingdom of heaven. Whoever becomes
humble like this child is the greatest in the kingdom of heaven."
    Matthew 18:1-4 (NRSV)

Blessed be the God and Father of our Lord Jesus Christ, who according
to His great mercy has caused us to be born again to a living hope
through the resurrection of Jesus Christ from the dead, to *obtain* an inheritance *which is imperishable and undefiled and will not fade away,
reserved in heaven for you.*   *1 Peter 1:3-4*

But, as it is written, "what no eye has seen, nor ear heard, nor the human
heart conceived, what God has prepared for those who love him."
    1 Corinthians 2:9 (NRSV)

HEALING **JOURNAL**
leg 36 / purpose

Use this page to record your personal thoughts and reflections.

leg 36 / purpose

Use this page to record your special Bible verses that encourage you on the journey (verses need not be limited to the ones in this book).

HEALING **JOURNAL**
leg 37 / renewed vitality

Use this page to record your personal thoughts and reflections.

leg 37 / renewed vitality

Use this page to record your special Bible verses that encourage you on the journey (verses need not be limited to the ones in this book).

HEALING **JOURNAL**
leg 38 / intimacy

Use this page to record your personal thoughts and reflections.

leg 38 / intimacy

Use this page to record your special Bible verses that encourage you on the journey (verses need not be limited to the ones in this book).

HEALING **JOURNAL**
leg 39 / peace

Use this page to record your personal thoughts and reflections.

leg 39 / peace

Use this page to record your special Bible verses that encourage you on the journey (verses need not be limited to the ones in this book).

HEALING **JOURNAL**
leg 40 / heaven

Use this page to record your personal thoughts and reflections.

leg 40 / heaven

Use this page to record your special Bible verses that encourage you on the journey (verses need not be limited to the ones in this book).

APPENDIX

Rema is the Greek expression for God's Word as it applies to a specific life and situation. This is not to be confused with *logos,* the totality or complete counsel of Scripture. *Rema,* then, is that tender touch that comes when God applies a certain verse from the Bible to your unique situation or pain.

May you find this book to be a messenger of His great love for you as you travel the path of pain and promise. You are invited to experience the growing freedom of those who have gone before you as you find that, indeed, there is a balm in Gilead.

The Scripture references, which reflect each leg of your healing journey, may be used in the following ways:

Read out loud.   Some readers find it easier to understand and internalize a verse if the words are spoken out loud. If you are such a reader, take time alone to speak the words and allow yourself to hear and receive the truth and comfort of each affirmation.

Read silently.   Many will find that reading the verses silently will cause them to move more deeply into the heart and spirit. If you are such a reader, keep your promise book with you, for it will be a welcome aid when you need the peace of God's Word. Don't hesitate to write the date in the margin when a verse suddenly becomes a part of you. These notations will be an invaluable testimony to God's provision and healing power as the years go by.

For study.   For those with the time and desire to study each verse as it becomes personal, there are excellent marginal references in a number of Scripture translations. One might also invest in commentaries and books that address Greek or Hebrew word studies.

For meditation.   Most will want to be still and meditate on a particular verse. As a verse becomes *rema* to your heart, God begins to reveal its purpose and relation to your past adversity.

For memorization.   The majority of survivors will find it helpful to memorize verses of comfort and compassion as they take the road to recovery. Nothing relieves stress and strengthens the wounded heart like the truth and assurance of His love written forever in your memory.

The verses you choose to compile may be different from those spoken to others along the way. Each word of Scripture has been tailor-made by God for your individual healing process. Others may not understand why a particular passage speaks so strongly to your situation. Nevertheless, it is valid and priceless *rema* for *your* soul.

Hold tight to each word. Breathe them into your spirit and know that they are *His* tender Words to minister to *you* on *your* special journey.

For more information contact:

> Philippian Ministries, Inc.
> 8515 Greenville Ave., Suite 103
> Dallas, TX 75243

Another book by Lana Bateman, *God's Crippled Children,* may be purchased by sending $10.50 (check or money order), to the above address.

God's Crippled Children is the story of Lana's life and the issues that drew her to face her need for the healing journey. It also describes Philippian Ministries and how it was born, and tells stories of many others whose emotions have been touched by our Lord Jesus. You will find it to be a special blessing and encouragement as you travel your road to recovery.

FORGIVENESS

Expressing emotion
Letting go of the story
Giving up my right
           to hurt back.

I want to be whole
Jesus cleanse my soul
And unchain me at last
           from my past.

KAY KOCOUR